Notes for Neuro Navigators

from the same author

Autistic World Domination

How to Script Your Life

Jolene Stockman

ISBN 978 1 83997 444 1

eISBN 978 1 83997 445 8

of related interest

Looking After Your Autistic Self

A Personalised Self-Care Approach to Managing Your Sensory and Emotional Well-Being

Niamh Garvey

ISBN 978 1 83997 560 8

eISBN 978 1 83997 561 5

The Autism-Friendly Cookbook

Lydia Wilkins

ISBN 978 1 83997 082 5

eISBN 978 1 83997 083 2

The #ActuallyAutistic Guide to Advocacy

Step-by-Step Advice on How to Ally and Speak Up with Autistic People and the Autism Community

Jennifer Brunton Ph.D. and Jenna Gensic M.A.

ISBN 978 1 78775 973 2

eISBN 978 1 78775 974 9

Notes for Neuro Navigators

The Allies' Quick-Start Guide to Championing Neurodivergent Brains

Jolene Stockman

Jessica Kingsley Publishers
London and Philadelphia

First published in Great Britain in 2024 by Jessica Kingsley Publishers
An imprint of John Murray Press

A CIP catalogue record for this title is available from the British Library and the Library of Congress

ISBN 978 1 83997 868 5
eISBN 978 1 83997 869 2

Printed and bound in Great Britain by Clays Ltd

Jessica Kingsley Publishers' policy is to use papers that are natural, renewable and recyclable products and made from wood grown in sustainable forests. The logging and manufacturing processes are expected to conform to the environmental regulations of the country of origin.

Jessica Kingsley Publishers
Carmelite House
50 Victoria Embankment
London EC4Y 0DZ

www.jkp.com

John Murray Press
Part of Hodder & Stoughton Ltd
An Hachette Company

Contents

Introduction

You can't tell who's who by looking. Autism isn't always white-cis-male. It isn't always mouth-words. It isn't always flapping, mimicking, pacing, meltdown-shutdown, touch-avoiding, head-phone-wearing, maths genius. Except when it is.

Your job is not to spot us, diagnose us, label us, or fix us. Your job? Open your heart. Soften your eyes. Ask questions and listen to the answers. A diagnosis is not a prediction. It doesn't tell you what's possible. It doesn't change you, your colleague, your child, or your friend. It just opens up tricks and tools to thrive.

Disclaimer: Autistics, like all human beings, come in epically individualized packages. I'm one. Just one. One of many ones. I bring my story, my words and ideas, but when it comes to autism? The best thing you can do is to talk to (and more importantly, *listen to*) the autistics in your life. We are the experts in our own experience, in our own needs, and we are key to unlocking a world where all people are valued and supported. Not for what we can do, but for who we are.

Being autistic is full-on, but being in the life of someone who is autistic? This can be epic, world-changing love. It's like when your partner is vegetarian, and you change the way you do things. You put a filter on; you choose different restaurants, buy different food, you change the way you live and see the world. You avoid meat because you love that person. And when someone is autistic, the people who love them learn to do the same thing. They become sensitive to their surroundings. They tweak the world.

These are our neuro navigators, our loved ones, who change the world to help us navigate, be comfortable, survive. They dim the lights, change the channel, buy different clothing, prepare food carefully. Autistics do this for ourselves, but for us it's not a choice. Our preferences aren't whims or nice-to-have's, they're meticulously developed systems. They are necessities. When someone who is not neurodivergent respects and accepts our needs as matter of fact, with no resentment, it validates our humanity. It is everything. As a neuro navigator, you make an incredible difference.

Neuro navigators understand that autistic supports are ideals, not inconveniences. And this understanding influences every element of your communication – the attitude and language, right down to the micro-expressions and vocal changes. It becomes subconscious, oozing from every choice you make. As an individual, as a person with the power to affect other people with your words, actions, and expressions every single day, you can give people who see the world differently the gift of accepting who and how they are.

Don't take your normal for granted. Some of us are working really hard to pull it off.

Since sharing my diagnosis in a TEDx talk, I've presented all over the world from New Zealand to New York. And you know what I've learned? People are *over* the negative, deficit-based narrative; hey – don't get me wrong, they don't want toxic-positivity either. The yippy-skippy superpowers spin is true in many ways, but it isn't the whole picture. And in the end? Autistic or not, we actually all want the same things: a life that we love, respect for who we are, and strategies that work.

Like me, an entire generation of autistics are discovering their neurodivergent identity as adults. Usually this is either due to a breakdown after years of exhausting themselves to fit in, something that's called 'masking', or a side-effect of having their own children diagnosed. The process of identifying traits makes their own childhood feel suddenly all too familiar. Apparently, I like to learn the hard way, so I went down the have-a-breakdown route. (One star, do not recommend.) I had always been called oversensitive, negative, and miserable, I had always experienced 'social hangovers' and been uncomfortable around people. Looking back now, I can see that my life had been repeated cycles of over-doing to prove myself, and then retreating to recover. Overwhelm then exhaustion. Trying to be normal, failing. Every time, thinking it was my fault, my problem, an innate brokenness in me. It wasn't until I felt physically out of control that I started worrying it could be something bigger.

I was at a shopping centre, during the worst possible time (lunch hour during school holidays) but I don't think it's as much the specifics of that day as it was an accumulation of stress over time. It was years and years of pushing down feelings, ignoring flashing engine lights, internal raging against a world that felt hopelessly rigged against me. The triggers from that day were small, comparatively: a jostling crowd, a laughing teen, a shiny floor, yellow balloons, a wind-up toy on a bursting sale shelf. Small on their own, but for me they represented breaking point. My heart thudded in my ears, my breathing slowed. Something inside me just...left. My physical carcass stayed behind, it couldn't move, bones heavy, muscles frozen. I couldn't speak, throat gone, mouth numb. My thinking, usually three hundred miles an hour, had slowed down so much I could barely instruct my breath. It was like a death without dying. My body was here, but I was gone. My husband got me home and to bed, I eventually recovered. But unlike every other cycle of exhaustion and recovery, this one scared me. This time felt dangerous. After months of researching nervous breakdowns and various tumours, I referred myself to the mental health department. Nothing new there, I already had my long-term companions major depressive disorder and generalized anxiety neatly diagnosed. However, this time was different. I had the incredible luck (and privilege) to be assigned a psychologist who was familiar with the different ways autism presents across genders. To her, the constellation created by my different stories and traits was clear: autism.

When I was first diagnosed, I was angry and scared, I didn't like that there was a word, a diagnosis even, for the things about me that I had been called all my life: oversensitive, weird, different. Eventually, I worked through the rollercoaster of emotions and the mountains of information. I learned that sooo much of what we think we know about autism is wrong, and I realized that the diagnosis gave me the language to describe how I felt, and gave me access to a community I had never had before. Suddenly, my differences gave me something I had never had before – a sense of belonging.

For me? The biggest advantage of being autistic and late-diagnosed is that I have the privilege of walking between worlds, the neurotypical and the neurodivergent, the diagnosed and the undiagnosed. The same way I reconcile my

Indigenous and colonizing DNA, I acknowledge that my intersectionality gifts me the ability (and the responsibility) to bridge worlds. *Āniwaniwa tū wae rua*, the legs of the rainbow stand in two different places.

In Aotearoa New Zealand, the native tītoki tree buds into glossy red berries. But not consistently. Not regularly. Not even predictably. And while the kōwhai and the pōhutukawa trees bloom, feeding hungry summer birds with flowers and berries, the tītoki does no such thing. The tītoki grows quietly, in its own way, glimmering with bright, shiny leaves.

There are tītoki trees that fruit every year, some only in winter, others that haven't for as long as people can remember, yet... The tītoki blooms in its own space, in its own time. Like every child, like every person, perfectly.

Interpreter and Māori language expert Keri Opai[1] coined the phrase *He wā tōna ka puāwai mai te tītoki*, the tītoki tree blooms in its own time.

Like every kind of 'different', autistics have always existed. We were the fire-watchers, the sensitives. We were the ones who perceived things others didn't, knew things others couldn't. So many of our Indigenous cultures light the way, embracing different as vital, and not in a patronizing 'every person is unique' kind of way, but with a deep, true respect for the qualities brought to our planet by every being in existence.

In Aotearoa New Zealand, a te reo Māori way of expressing autism is *takiwātanga*, meaning in his/her/my/their own space and time. Again, developed by Keri Opai, and adopted by people across the world as a definition that resonates, because the medical definition of autism, as well as being hideously deficit-based, divides us in its contradictions, inaccurate functioning labels, autistic traits framed as symptoms, and preferences labelled shortfalls. *Takiwātanga* gives us an expression that uplifts our dignity and individuality. Yes, we are all autistic, even when some of us don't use words and others are hyperlexic, even when some of us like tight hugs and small spaces, and others find touch painful. Within our different needs, strengths, challenges, preferences, and privileges, we are all autistic, *takiwātanga*, we all have a very different way of experiencing and being in the world.

Make way, ADHD! I do not have a deficit or a disorder. Instead? *Aroreretini*, my attention flies to many things. Hyperactivity is your experience of me. At my end? I am excited, filled with energy and hungry to direct it. I have ideas and passion, and the rest of the world is just... So. Slow. Join me! Or stay out of my way! Same traits, different points of view. Indigenous language is innately strengths-based, and I am grateful for the work being done in this space. You can see more of Keri Opai's beautiful Māori language work in the online glossary at www.tereohapai.nz.

Over time, I've learned to block out a lot of the things that hurt me. I've learned how to grit my teeth and get through it. I've learned how to hide it. When I mask, my autism isn't gone. It's just no longer anyone else's problem. I'm working to exhaustion to fit in with others, with the majority. And I don't mean to complain – I made it, I'm a grown-up. I don't even do it consciously any more. It's not a switch I control, although I do know when it's on. I mean, if you could be beautiful by concentrating really hard, you'd give it a go. And when you got a good reaction, you'd keep it up. Masking doesn't feel like a choice; little by little, it becomes who you are.

So, I mimic normal by pretending things don't hurt, that they don't make my skin crawl. Light: Nothing bright, nothing sudden. Sound: Nothing loud, nothing unexpected. Nothing monotonous, grating, or scrapey. Then there's textures, food, clothing, furniture. I have developed a whole lot of rules about a whole lot of things. For example: Being early to events to ease my anxiety, a high ratio of downtime to 'out' time, eliminating entire food groups, etc., etc. As you can imagine, it makes me really fun to live with. #Sarcasm.

As neuro navigators, my family understand that these rules aren't me being picky or difficult, they love me enough to trust that I need these things to be okay. The way they treat me isn't impacted by my needs. And no, even telling people my rules doesn't help, because then they make a big deal out of it, become morbidly curious, or just can't *not* comment. Every time. Why can't my sensory needs be as matter of fact as someone else's allergies or dietary requirements? Look, I don't want to be patronized, babied, or tolerated. When people tiptoe around me, I feel so self-conscious, I want to shiver away into nothing. Far easier for me to suck it up, mask, and get through it.

So here's the trick: Trust the autistic. When we say something hurts, it hurts. When we say it's too loud, it's too loud. Chances are? Autistic adults will only tell you once. We are so used to being ignored or argued with that we won't spend energy trying to convince you, we will use it to mask instead.

Masking can include: scripting and practising conversations; pretending not to be anxious or overwhelmed; not stimming in public; faking or forcing eye contact and facial expressions; over-analysing interactions; talking too much; acting interested or comfortable; hiding passions and interests; pushing through discomfort; only using supports in private (e.g. fidgets, weighted blankets, headphones, sunglasses, etc.); copying other people (e.g. style, clothing, speech, gestures, body language, etc.).

Long-term masking can lead to autistic burnout. Many autistics experience regular periods of burnout throughout their lives but may not realize what it is, putting it down to their own weakness or a stressful life event. When we know that burnout is common for autistics, we can learn the warning signs, alleviate symptoms, soften the environments that trigger them. Imagine a world where being autistic is simply another way of life. Not a medically diagnosed disorder. A globally embraced culture. (Not to mention that all humans would benefit from more focus on greater self-care and understanding.)

Autistics can't get back the time we've lost, the energy, the opportunities. But we can start now. We can give ourselves the identity, the understanding, and the power to create the world we deserve.

Often, when I speak to groups, a parent will come up to me afterwards and say, 'I hope my [autistic] kid turns out like you!' But I don't want that, and I tell them so. Don't get me wrong, I'm happy now and life is awesome, but it's taken far more energy, time, and courage than I would ever recommend. Because if I had been identified earlier, supported, and accepted, I wouldn't be here now. I would be a truer version of myself, probably happily mute, definitely living quietly, and possibly using a pseudonym #Haha.

On the upside, now I get to use all the consequences of not being diagnosed or labelled, all the exhausting side-effects of fighting who I am to blend into the regular world (I can speak! I can leave the house!) to make it different for the autistics coming up behind me. I'm grateful now, for the ability and the opportunity to speak. So much work to train myself, to go against my instincts. But do I want it for the little ones that follow me? No. Your voice matters, you deserve to be heard. But not at the cost of who you are.

Obviously, as an allistic (non-autistic) you can't know what you don't know, but you can make it easier. It's an attitude, an openness, a curiosity. It's believing that there is more than one right way to be human. If you believe, on any level, in any way, that autistics (or neurodivergents of any flavour) are less-than? You will ooze it. Your words, actions, and even your face will give you away.

For me, belonging in this world would be not holding my breath, not holding back, not sitting tight and clenched and bracing for the next hurt. As an autistic, I'm having a pretty intense day-to-day experience, I'm sensing things more intensely, taking in environmental signals, and probably working really hard to not let on that I am working really hard. What this means is that things that can be everyday for a typical brain can set off a stress response for me. Like lots of autistics I have high anxiety, so I worry-think-overthink... True belonging, to me, would be a freedom from anxiety, freedom from fear, and feeling accepted as I am, finally able to breathe.

So many autistics have had difficult relationships, with people in general, and with loved ones particularly. We carry trauma from being misunderstood, by our families, authority figures, even ourselves. So many of us come into adulthood without a diagnosis, and so may not even realize why or how we are. This is where you come in! Not because you have to spot or diagnose us. Don't do that. (Seriously, don't do that.*) But because you get to be someone who comes into the relationship with total respect and openness.

Before we get into the challenges, tips, and theories, if you hear nothing else from me, hear this: You are doing a great job. The fact that you're here, learning and working to be better, means that you care. You're open and listening. That is everything.

So, welcome. Thank you for being here, for learning our culture and language, and for understanding how to help autistics navigate the current world, while supporting us to build a new one. Autistics need you to know that they are amazing exactly as they are, and to believe it. We need this because often we can't see it in ourselves. You are absolutely the best person to support the autistic in your life, to be their

* And I know, it can be sooooo hard to hold back when you think you've spotted an autistic in the wild, and they (or the people around them) have no idea. And I'd say it's about a *million* times harder when it's family. Luckily, all the strategies for making the world easier will work whether you say, 'We do this because [person's name] is autistic' or, 'We do this because it works for [person's name].' So, you can suggest or implement autism-friendly strategies without ever using the a-word if they're not ready to hear or use it.

partner, parent, teacher, loved one, friend, or professional, but they are the best person to know, understand, and be themselves.

Here we go, neuro navigators, this one's for you. We'll kick it off with a run-down of the basics.

Identity and Language

For many people, being autistic is an identity. As important as nationality, ethnicity, ability status, or writing hand. This identity is a lens through which we see and experience the world. Autism does not need to be cured or fixed, because we are not sick or broken.

A child's true self is not *buried under* their autism, a tween is not *burdened with* or *suffering from* their identity, an adult didn't *recover from* their autism. Being autistic is an integral part of who we are. Honouring identity is important not just for autistic people, but for our entire world as we move into more conscious and deliberate ways of speaking and being.

I know analysing our language is super-sensitive and may seem small or trivial. But what if something as simple as changing our language could change the way a person sees themselves? Sees the world? *He mana tō te kupu,* words have power.

Right now, if you are a parent or professional, you are the source of language for your child. So, until they're old enough to decide, you will shape who they are with the words you use. Just ask yourself why you are using the language you choose. If you believe a child is less-than, the child will feel that from you, with your words and your energy around them.

For example: Is your child *picky and difficult*, or *selective and specific*? These sound like tiny changes, and they are, but over time, language builds a person's image of who they are and what they think is possible for them.

Picky and *selective*, technically, mean the same thing; but *picky* reeks of judgement and negativity; *selective* feels deliberate and empowering. Consider what your child hears you say about them, and about autism. I wish I had overheard people saying, 'Yes, she's super-sensitive and knows exactly what she likes' rather than, 'Urgh, she's just oversensitive and difficult.'

Your beliefs colour the words you use. And your beliefs and values can be so deeply ingrained that your language is unconsciously skewed. But whether you know it or not, you ooze who you are and what you believe. So, get conscious, dig deep: What is true for you? What do you believe?

- Do you understand and believe in the strengths of neurodiversity?
- Do you respect the independence and power of all autistics?
- Do you feel optimistic and excited about the future for autistics?

You are a grown-up. You have the power to change your mind, and you can give yourself permission to do so. Start questioning your existing beliefs and start creating beliefs that empower you and the people around you.

People say, 'We don't want to label the child, it'll make them feel different.' Spoiler alert: Neurodivergents know they're different. A label just lets us know that our differences are okay. That we belong here exactly as we are. Personally, I'm not used to having my differences accepted with kindness. Either from others or myself. That's one of the biggest things I've learned since going public with my autistic identity: the ripple effects of autism on the individual – anxiety, depression, withdrawal – these are not a part of autism. These are the consequences of society's intolerance of 'other' and our own fear of not belonging.

Your autistic child will grow into an autistic adult. Consider this: Are you a parent? Or a person with children? Sit with this for a moment. If someone referred to you as *a person with children*, how would you feel? It's different to being called a *parent*, right? Subtle, but distinctly detached. This is the difference between saying someone is *autistic* and saying someone *has autism*.

Research shows that identity-first language ('I'm an autistic person') is overwhelmingly preferred by autistic adults, but if you're not sure, just ask. Society is growing and evolving (and that's a good thing!), and new language lets us honour and describe these changes. If you love words and language (like me!) and it's fun for you, you can commit to learning about the history and development of new words, or, here's the shortcut: just be respectful and kind. Ask and listen. Language preferences are not for you to argue, they are there for you to accept and use.

Always. If someone shares themselves with you, respect and honour that. A person's identity, pronouns, name, or title are not up for debate. Please understand that if we explain ourselves, we are trading our energy for your education. Honour that gift. Many of us are tired, and it can often be less energy to mask our hurt feelings than to fight an onslaught of ignorance.

Identity isn't always straightforward or even accessible. Someone may be neurodivergent and not feel comfortable sharing their diagnosis (not that they should have to share anything to be respected or treated well), or they may be neurodivergent and not know it themselves. So, what does this mean for neuro navigators? It means a formal diagnosis, visible disability, or even asking for help cannot be, and should not be, how we determine the supports in place.

And as for your own kids? Right now, you have a lot of power. You decide the language they hear and, until they decide otherwise, use. If you tell your friends, 'No, we can't come it's just too hard *with her autism*,' your child will hear you. What you said and what it means for them. They will translate your excuse into condemnation of a part of them they know they can't change. You will plant seeds in your child, not to hate autism, but to hate themselves.

Your children will grow into adults, they will eventually do their own learning, make their own decisions. But right now? You can be brave, maybe even uncomfortable at first, but you can gift them the language their community prefers. And who knows, you might even realize that autistic world domination is best for everyone!

A note on neurodiversity*

Neurodiversity is a biological characteristic of human beings. The word was coined by Australian Judy Singer in 1998 and it is the understanding that humans are diverse, varied, in our brain function.

> Neurodiversity names a biological reality, the virtually infinite neuro-cognitive variability within Earth's human population. It points to the fact that every human has a unique nervous system with a unique combination of abilities and needs. That is all. – Judy Singer[2]

Neurodiversity is some people running on Linux, other people on Windows, some on Mac, others using a combination of systems, and still others programming completely new systems from scratch. We are all neurodiverse. But what about those of us with a brain that isn't typical? Autistic, hyperactive, dyslexic, with mental health issues, post-traumatic stress, epilepsy... all of us who have brains that differ in some way from what is (supposedly) the majority. Kassiane Asasumasu** coined the words neurodivergence and neurodivergent. She says,

---

* Reprinted from my book *Autistic World Domination: How to Script Your Life*, Jessica Kingsley Publishers, 2023.

** Kassiane Asasumasu is a multiply neurodivergent Hapa (biracial Asian) neurodiversity activist. Read more at www.divergentminds.org/about

'neurodivergent refers to neurologically divergent from typical',[3] and this includes innate and acquired neurodivergence.

- **Innate neurodivergence:** This is neurodivergence a person is born with, such as autism, hyperactivity, dyslexia, dyscalculia, giftedness, sensitivity, and Tourette's. Indigeneity (see the box below) is another key innate neurodivergence.

Different ethnicities, nationalities, and cultures bring different ways of seeing and experiencing the world. Indigenous minds are often more in tune with the environment, they connect and communicate in distinct and significant ways. This innate neurodivergence holds strong even through many generations of colonization.

- **Acquired neurodivergence:** Neurodivergence a person takes on from trauma, culture, long-term meditation, or mental health challenges. This neurodivergence features boosted creativity and empathy. It offers a unique way of experiencing the world. People in the Deaf and Blind communities may also identify as neurodivergent.

Neurodiversity is biological, natural, and more than that: valuable. Harnessing the skills and energy of neurodiversity is the key to innovation, to greater empathy and understanding. Understanding neurodiversity is key to the new world.

You Are Not Alone

Community

As a neuro navigator, you are not alone. When you're ready, identify ways you can connect yourself, your child, or your family. Connect with people who get it – the neurodivergents who have survived, the neuro navigators who are still learning. Because that is what will resonate with you. It's what will save you. The stories. The successes. There are people on the same journey as you, with the same challenges and adventures. People and families who live in the kind of parallel world that you see and feel, and who are figuring it out, too. It's these people who will make the difference. With their open hearts, soft non-judgey eyes, people who take the time to slow down, understand, to ask questions and to care. You will realize that being wired up differently only makes someone different, not wrong. And that there are sooo many of us!

Heads up: Community may not be perfect. It also may not be who you expect. Not everyone has the heart or capacity to take this journey. Your closest friends may fade out of your life, your family may become a source of hurt. Know that you are not alone in these hard changes, either.

You can find support community:

- **Online:** Join online groups or mailing lists. And you don't have to spill your guts to feel better! Lurk if you prefer. Even just reading will give you tips, acknowledgement, and encouragement that you are not alone.
- **In real life:** Get in touch with autistic-led autism organizations or informal support groups. Meeting others like you will reassure you and provide opportunities to breathe.

The hashtag #ActuallyAutistic will let you find information from autistics themselves. Non-autistic professionals, families, and friends can provide information and support, but they cannot speak for autistics or from an autistic point of view.

You are not alone, far from it, you are part of a huge community of people who are making a difference. Because autistics are beautiful, super-sensitive beings, but we are in a world where right now we're still getting told to 'harden up' and 'get over it' – and you can be our safe place. As parents, as adults, as role-models, as important people in an autistic's life, you can help give us the gift of knowing and accepting who we are, knowing that there are strengths in our differences and that you are here to help us figure them out. That way, instead of fighting a world designed for neurotypicals, autistics can spend our time and energy building a happy life in a world that is truly ours.

Role-models

As a kid, I never saw anyone like me, all I knew was that I was oversensitive, weird, and different; I couldn't handle things, so I spent a lot of energy either pretending to fit in or hating myself for being so broken and useless. In many ways, I'm kind of jealous of the autistics who express their overwhelm outwardly, because they are harder to ignore. They kick and scream against the what-is. They fight with every cell. And even though they may not know exactly what help they need, they know that something is wrong with the world, and they won't stop until they are heard.

And whether we exhaust ourselves fighting or protect ourselves masking, it all changes when we are reflected in the world around us. So, until we are heard? We need more autistic role-models: parents, teachers, nurses, administrators, autistics in every profession, everywhere! People who see the world in the same way we do and can change the way the systems see us.

Autistic role-models show us different ways of being in the world. They show us that we belong. They offer connection, understanding, and they show us what's possible. Stories and role-models are far more powerful than statistics and predictions.

- **In person:** Social or support groups.
- **Online:** Groups or advocates.
- **Through positive media representation:** Books, TV shows, movies.

> When autistics are around other autistics, we know it. It lets us breathe in a way that is hard to explain, except I think it might be how neurotypicals feel all the time! An unconditional sense of belonging. Understood, accepted, part of the bigger picture.

As society has become more open to difference, autistic representation has increased. Autistic characters can be seen in television, movies, and books. In some ways, this is great:

- increased knowledge and awareness
- increased understanding and acceptance
- normalizing of autism and autistics.

In other ways, not so great:

- reinforced stereotypes
- increased misunderstanding
- increased prejudice.

Media representation opens doors. It provides opportunities to have conversations, ask questions, to learn, and to understand. Just remember: We're not all a socially incompetent genius, we're not all the quirky gamer or the awkward IT specialist, we don't all love trains, maths, or colour-coded candy. But we are all human, individual, and as deserving of love and respect as anyone else.

And when thinking about the autistics that you're lucky enough to come into contact with – remember that any changes you make, any learning you do for this child, this person, will make a difference to your own growth, to the effectiveness of your work, and ultimately, to our community and the world. Seriously. Autism-friendly is human-friendly.

Always ask autistics

When it comes to autistic-focused supports, the golden rule is *nothing about us, without us.** Ask autistics, be led by autistics. And I don't mean putting the burden on individuals within your circle or organization; they may already be stressed, overwhelmed, misdiagnosed, or undiagnosed, they may not feel confident to share their needs, they may not know what supports are possible or have the words to ask for them. It's not good enough to say, 'If someone asks for accommodations, we'll do it.'

Instead? Do your own research. Check in with other people and organizations, hire neurodivergent consultants, find what is working for autistics out in the world. Be proactive, make strategies available for everyone. Autism-friendly is human-friendly. Don't wait for suggestions or issues to come up, anticipate, and then offer suggestions. Educate yourself. Sometimes suggesting options that have worked for other people can help normalize support needs (while not making an individual feel less-than or weird). For example: 'I've had other students who found the quiet room really useful at lunchtimes' or 'Some of the sales team find it easier to focus with headphones.'

---

* This is the main principle and call of the Disability Rights Movement.

In the new world, universal design and universal supports (we'll talk more about this later!) will mean that humans of every neurotype, every ability, and every kind of magic are affirmed in all kinds of ways. Not because of special programmes or extra supports, but because the default systems are open, respectful, and flexible. Let's head towards that by looking at some strategies for autistics to navigate the neurotypical world.

Strategies

Hey there, if you skipped reading the rest of the book, and came straight here, it's okay. You're looking for the tricks, right? The shortcuts, the how-to's. You're looking for the best ways to help the autistic in your life. Help them, fix them, control them. You're taking the initiative, good for you.

Happily, you can make a huge difference to any autistic, and we'll look at lots of ways you can do that starting now! However, before we begin, I have to break it to you: You're probably the one that needs to change #SorryNotSorry.

All of the things autistics do that worry/annoy/embarrass/anger the neurotypical people around them, *are perfectly normal for autistics*. Being autistic is a special and specific way of being in and experiencing the world. And if that's all you get from this book, that's awesome. (But hey, if you get inspired to read more and understand more, even better!)

Autistics do not need to be fixed. Autistics are not broken. What we do need are tools and strategies to navigate the neurotypical world, and ways to discover our strengths and passions.

Your ideas, words, and actions teach the people around you. You can teach autistics that they need to cover their sensitivities to make other people comfortable, or you can teach them to trust their bodies, accept their sensitivities, and strategize their challenges. I know, it's a lot. But you have the privilege of these things being a choice for you. Autistics don't have that choice. Read that again: You have the privilege of choice. Autistics don't. And that is why your support and understanding is huge.

Many adult autistics have had a lifetime of difficult relationships. We carry trauma from being misunderstood – by our families, authority figures, even ourselves. So many of us walk the world trying to 'pull off' normal, working to prove our worth against a constant gnawing fear of being scorned or rejected. We have a strong sense of feeling different and unwanted for the things we do, say, and feel – for being who we are. Every autistic adult has a head full of childhood memories and experiences that confirm this. Disapproving stares. Embarrassed family members placating irritated strangers. This is where you come in! You need to let go of any idea of normal. You need to up your tolerance for weird. Get over it. Get onboard. Get the judgey out of your eyes. Because no autistic is judged or bullied for being autistic. We're judged and bullied for the way we talk, the way we work, the things we like, for being different, for being *weird*. This means it's not enough to say you are an ally. It's not enough to know the words and tick the boxes. This is about you. You ooze how you feel. And the way you hold yourself in every moment lets us know whether you truly believe we are okay, or not okay.

So, here's your strategy: Control everything you think and say, your behaviour, and how you come across to everyone around you. Again, I know it sounds like a lot, but [shrugs] it's what you have to do. Okay, so I'm kidding (kind of).

But right now? This is exactly what society expects from autistics. We are required to appear neurotypical. We are punished for being ourselves, rewarded for fighting our instincts. We are pressured to make ourselves acceptable by conforming to an arbitrary 'normal' that makes us miserable. And why? For your comfort. Seriously.

- Making eye contact is not a requirement of listening, it is not proof of honesty. It is a neurotypical preference.
- Making small talk is not a universal human experience, it is not an innate skill. It is a neurotypical nicety.
- Taking your words literally is not a sign of faulty understanding or poor social skills. It is direct autistic communication.
- Holding your body in quiet, tidy ways is not written on the box we came in. The way the human body moves is individual and neuro-specific.

The default system is currently neurotypical. You may not have created this system, but you benefit from it. Step one is to become conscious of your neurotypical privilege. This privilege allows you to walk the world in comfort, with (for the most part) your sensory and communication needs understood and met.

Privilege is the advantage of *not* having an obstacle. We all have privilege. If you can see without glasses? Privilege. Grew up with a supportive family? Privilege.

Privilege works both ways – a high-masking autistic has the privilege of choosing whether or not to share their identity, while a low-masking autistic has the privilege of not having their identity doubted or questioned. Appreciate all the ways you quietly benefit in this world, and notice how others quietly struggle. Considering your privilege keeps you both humble and grateful.

If you're right-handed and your friends are all left-handed, you're the one that sticks out. But when you go home and most of your family are right-handed, it's just normal. Okay, so then what's normal? Normal is whatever we are used to. Whatever there is *most* of. The bulk, the herd, the majority. The current world is designed for average people. Typical people. And here's the opportunity: To create a world that empowers all humans by focusing on the least typical and most challenged people, a world that works for every type of human. We've got to do more than just appreciate difference and celebrate diversity. We have to be willing to change our own expectations and norms so that difference and diversity *is* the expectation. We have more information, technology, and trinkets than we've ever dreamed of. But now it's time to create a world that is neuro-affirming for all brains.

This is your opportunity to step up. To be the person in a child's life who validates their experience and confirms that their feelings are not only real, but that they matter. Someone who gets to provide the (seemingly simple but sadly rare) gift of allowing a child to be exactly who they are without judgement or expectation. It is *everything* to support a child to trust themselves and to know that there is more than one way to be human. Many autistics grow up feeling alone, and I promise you one person, one interaction, one moment of light in that darkness, can be what keeps us here. (And just because something works for other people, doesn't mean it's the best or right way for everyone!)

Warning: Be careful of strategies that encourage or aim to help an autistic to become neurotypical. When you try to teach an autistic to think, act, and appear 'normal', we will not be happier or better off; instead, we will learn:

- Our feelings aren't real.
- We can't trust our bodies.
- Our needs don't matter.
- You don't see / care who we really are.
- Pretending to be neurotypical (masking) makes the people around us happy.

Before you put any strategy in place, consider: What is the ideal outcome of this strategy? Who is it for? Really? Remember that being or appearing 'normal' should never be the goal of a strategy. The goal is to support a happy, confident, joyous autistic!

Safety

When human beings don't feel safe, there is a physical response, a chemical reaction in our bodies. To autistics, threats can be sensory or social challenges, changes to expectations or routine, or any other of a million different stressors.

Autistics have their own personalized hierarchy of needs and will focus on their most pressing need (usually safety) before being able to move up the hierarchy. For example: I barely ate at school. I was using all my physical and emotional energy to survive the social, mental, emotional, and sensory onslaught. At school, my body didn't even register food as a need. Chewing, swallowing, and digesting nutrients while I was surrounded by people was not even my body's lowest priority.

The first priority for autistics is almost always safety. Easing anxiety. Preventing teasing or rejection. It might not be the traditional definition of safety, no our life isn't in danger, but physically our body processes it just as seriously. We are anxious, threatened, and looking for peace. How can you help an autistic feel safe?

Here are some ideas to build a sense of safety:

- **Home:** Home is our safe place. Know that home may be the only place where an autistic can be ourselves. Give us the space and unconditional love we need to recover from the stressors of the outside world.
- **Grounding:** Meditation, time in nature, learning to swim, climbing walls or trees, a trampoline, a swing, a quiet corner. Routine and traditions.
- **Connection:** Invite us. We want to be included, even if it doesn't always seem that way. Even if we say no every time, the act of inviting us to join you in your world (to eat at the table, to come on a walk, to visit the relatives, to after work events, etc.) is enough. Asking lets us know that we are important to you. Invite us to join you and (here's the trick) be truly okay if we say no. Don't stop asking. And meanwhile?

Join us. If we're playing Minecraft, pull up a chair. If we're reading a book, read too. If we're lying on the floor, join us. Our world is different to yours but no less special. Autistics are not wired to look for ulterior motives or to judge your worth. We sense your truth, and you don't have to earn your place with us, being present is enough.

Objects that connect us to home or our favourite places can help remind us that we have a safe place. This can include small toys or objects, jewellery with special meaning, quotes or lists on paper, routines and traditions that connect us to people, time, and events.

- **Making the unknown known:** Easing transitions (more on this later!), establishing and maintaining routine and familiarity. We need detail with straightforward language, and time to process information. We need to feel okay to ask questions, so be ready to have the status quo challenged. Can you open your mind? See the world fresh? Because you will find that right now, human beings do a lot of things 'because it's the way it's always been done' and not necessarily because it is the most efficient or effective way. Can you set your ego aside? Can you change?
- **Managing expectations:** No surprises. Autistics need to know what is happening, when, how, where, and who will be there. This is so we can prepare. Obviously, life is unpredictable, but we can create certainties. Do your best. Tell the truth. Use phrases like 'If anything changes, I'll let you know as soon as

I do' or 'Sometimes things change, but we'll figure it out together.'

Even understanding and acknowledging frustration can help defuse the emotion: 'We weren't expecting it to rain, and now we have to change our plans and be inside. That's so frustrating!' Make success possible by keeping demands and pressure low. For example: 'We'll go in, and if we're not feeling okay after ten minutes, we'll go home.' Let them know that it will be win-win: 'If there's no food you like at the lunch, we will get a drive-thru on the way home.' (And don't just say it, actually mean it, and when required, do it.)

- **Food:** Here's the thing, the repetition, the sameness, the consistency... With food it's often (again!) all about safety. Food means being able to take a break from my brain screaming at me with fight or flight (or freeze, flop, or friend/fawn), being able to rest my mind that's always looking for hazards and threats, which as an autistic, I sense everywhere. Even while my face is straight. You know how the autistic you know seems like they're not paying attention, but you know they heard every word you said (and will quote you later). Autistics pick up on a million little things that no one else does. It's our superpower and our kryptonite – to be so magically, painfully, overwhelmingly sensitive, that sitting to eat something fairly plain, probably with my back to a wall, or in a small dark space, is comforting.

  When I get a cheeseburger combo with Coke and

extra sauce, the bag is the same – folded the same, smells the same, it looks the same, it makes the same comforting rustles, I can eat it in exactly the same way each time, alternating the three items the way I like to. I know it will be the same number of bites, the same ratio of textures. This sameness, this consistency, gives me something that the everyday life does not: reliability. I can trust processed food. I can trust white rice, hot fries, plain cheese. No surprises. No changes. I can eat it and I can breathe. Appreciate the importance of food for us.

- **Assuming competence and positive intention:** Behaviours are communication. Autistics are always trying to stay happy and safe, *whatever it may look like to you*. Read that again, because it's a big one. Autistics are often seen as 'the bad one', 'the troublemaker', or worse, when we just tend to be the ones who are unafraid to speak up or 'make a scene'. So, before you speak or assume, before you take action, take a breath. Consider any possible positive intention the autistic may have, and *act as though that is the truth*. Worst case, you have one less negative interaction. Best case (and what will happen most often), a positive intention *is* the truth.

  For example: An autistic child being rough with their classmates: 'You want to play with the other kids! I wonder if there's a way you can play that is gentle?' or when they interrupt others, 'I can see that you have something to share! Can you show me how we take turns?' And with autistic adults? It's the same idea: 'I know how hard it is for you to come out with me, is there a way we could make it easier?' or, 'You've been at work all day, you must be so over people. How about we plan for some people-free time gaming next weekend?'

- **Personal safety:** Knowing ourselves, understanding boundaries (how to put them in place, and how to protect them), being able to say what we need and be heard. This can be especially hard for adult autistics who have spent much of their life trying to make other people happy. Learning to put ourselves first can be challenging. Here's where neuro navigators come in! You can help us learn to trust our bodies in a world where we can be called everything from 'tactless and rude' to 'oversensitive' (and often in the same interaction). But please don't train us to look to you for affirmation. You won't always be around. Tell us...
  - 'You can trust your body.'
  - 'If it doesn't feel right to you, then it's not right.'
  - 'I support you and I will back you up in any way that makes this easier for you.'

...and then keep your word. If we say *it hurts*, believe us. If we say *it's true*, consider it objectively. Let your first response be to affirm and acknowledge that we know ourselves best.

Make trusting our bodies and practising boundaries part of the everyday, make sure we know:

- We have a right to say no.
- We have a right to change our minds (at any point).

- We have a right to ask for any time or space that we need to process.

Do it with minor things (outings, food, clothing) to strengthen our muscles for major things (life choices, health, and relationships).

Autistics are innately vulnerable and trusting. This puts us in danger, at risk of manipulation and abuse. When people we love teach us to conform under pressure (whether a disapproving eye-roll or withheld approval), what chance do we have against harmless strangers? Selfish friends? Abusers?

It is also critical to role-model this yourself and remember: For us, people-pleasing is a poison, and you are not an exception. *You* need to respect our boundaries. *You* need to hear our 'no'. *You* need to have no doubt that our decisions have weight, so you can teach us that we have power.

People describe living with autistics as 'walking on eggshells' and in a way, it is. The people around us (the ones who care) become conscious of our sensitivities and work hard to support us. Yes, it's exhausting – but it's exhausting for us, too. And we don't have a choice. For many autistics, the only thing worse than the onslaught of our environment is knowing that you are a problem or an issue to the people around you. We would rather mask, we would rather hurt ourselves. Try to think of it as finding balance, as fine-tuning the world. When a neurodivergent brain feels safe, it spends less energy on anxiety and handling the world. This free energy unlocks the magic.

Safe spaces

Anxiety is huge for autistics. Basically, it means any time we're out in the world, we're holding our breath, dealing with an almost constant sense of fight or flight (or freeze, flop, or friend/fawn, if you want all the options).

This means that home is our safe place. The place where we can breathe, and stamp, and cry, or sleep off the stress of the outside world. Home is our rock in the ocean, *he toka tū moana*, with people who will love us, even when we push them away.

So, what does this look like for the neuro navigators? Autistic adults can be on edge all day, masking and holding themselves together. They may then come home exhausted, shut off, shut down, disappear into a comfort activity (sleep, food, gaming, etc.). Or maybe you have an autistic child who melts down after school. They get in the car, in the door, and the tears start, the rage, the kicking, screaming, or the tuning out, the grogginess, the sleeping. I know you think you want a kid that comes home and is all, 'Mother, Father, I'm home! I've had the most marvellous day!' The truth is? That makes *you* feel better, not them. The truth is: Life is hard, harder when you're autistic, and harder still when you're an autistic kid and have such little control of your world. Don't be another person we have to perform for.

As an autistic kid who didn't know it, I trained myself to modify my truth to be acceptable, to be normal. Except when I got home and was too exhausted and miserable to pretend. As a loved one, you just want to fix it, make things better, but that's got to be long term. Short term? Please don't make it worse.

Acknowledge our reality. Support us with acceptance,

not with meaningless platitudes like, 'Everyone has days like that' or 'It's not that bad.' When you do this, it diminishes our experience and teaches us that you can't handle our truth. Instead? Pause, breathe. Hear us, hold space for us. 'I can see it's been a hard day for you. I'll get you [insert food/object/comfort] and let's just sit together.' Show us that our truth doesn't scare you, teach us that we don't have to pretend to make you happy. Let it be okay for things to not be okay.

So, yes, autistics can be different at home than at work or school. This doesn't mean we're faking or being naughty or manipulative, or any of the other autism myths. Remember, no matter how it looks from the outside, whether we're kicking, thrashing, snapping, shutting down, we're truly, truly, focused on easing our anxiety and creating safety. We are doing everything we can to survive and navigate a world that is not designed for us.

You, your home, your office, or your classroom can be an autistic's safe place. The place where they aren't judged or doubted. Believe me, we get plenty of that everywhere else. You get to be someone who gets them, who sees them.

Setting up (and keeping!) expectations makes a huge difference. It's about overload. You won't always know which sensory sensitivities affect the autistic you're with – but you can create an environment where they feel comfortable expressing their needs.

I was a straight-A, friendly, no-problem student. I always went above and beyond with my work, I figured out what people needed from me and gave it to them. But it cost me, and it hurt me. I cried so much as a kid that people stopped asking me what the matter was. How could I explain, it was everything?

For an autistic, so much of the world is uncomfortable. Sensory input, routine, rules. We learn that things other people find easy, are difficult for us. We learn that if we want an outcome (survival, love, comfort etc.), we've got to push through the discomfort. And ultimately? We learn that how we feel and what we want don't matter. So, phrases like 'I'm not okay with this' or 'This doesn't feel right to me' get scrubbed out of our vocabulary. Can you imagine how vulnerable this makes autistics? Vulnerable to manipulation? Trauma? Violence? Unhappiness? Being taken advantage of? Supporting autistics to trust how we feel and express our needs is a safeguard, an act of love, and a potential lifesaver.

Sensory strategies

Because of the way my brain processes the world, I'm having a pretty intense everyday experience. To me, some sounds are louder, lights are brighter. Movement and water can be mesmerizing, textures distracting. I don't have a good sense of where my body is in space and I can mix up how it feels, so I'll misjudge distances and bump into things, wear the 'wrong' clothing (i.e. no shoes in winter, coats in summer), I have super-specific food preferences, and look awkward even when I'm the most comfortable. From the outside, none of these things are big, noticeable signs (otherwise I would've been diagnosed far earlier, and people wouldn't still say to me, 'You don't look autistic!'), but on the inside, all heaven (or hell) can be breaking loose, and I'm so used to covering it up, that (usually) you'd never know.

In a world that is constantly telling autistics: 'You're too sensitive', 'No one else can hear it', 'Are you sure?', 'Stop being difficult', or 'You'll be fine', a world that gaslights us until we can't believe our own minds, supporting autistics to trust our bodies, trust our senses is HUGE. And this can be as simple as believing us.

After that, it comes down to comfort and recovery.

Comfort

This is getting through the everyday, dealing with the near-constant sensory blitz, the sounds, smells, textures, lights of neurotypical life. This can be done in different ways that either dull or enhance our sensory and internal experience, depending on our preference.

- **Sound:** Headphones to either block or create sound.
- **Clothing:** Thoughtful textures and fastenings, seamless or tag-free clothing.
- **Light:** Sunglasses, a hat, or hood to ease sensory input.
- **Tools:** A device, pen and paper, fidgets, chewable necklace, weighted soft toy, wheat bag, etc.
- **Food:** Keep safe food available. Plan around meals, have favourites available, buy in bulk.
- **List and routines:** Knowing plans, routes, activities, and places in advance can help prepare for sensory challenges. For example, loud places, areas with strong smells, etc.

- **Flexibility:** Planning and consistency aren't always possible. So, an important strategy can be planting seeds to promote flexibility. When autistics understand that other people don't have the same needs and sensitivities, it can help us to let go (a little!). We can't always control the outside world, so sometimes we need ways to control ourselves. Create and repeat key phrases* that empower with flexibility. For example: 'I am practising being flexible.' 'When I try different things, I might find a new favourite.' 'This [sound/smell] is temporary.' 'Sometimes plans can change.' 'It's okay to change your mind.' 'People like different things/have different ideas, and that's okay.' 'Different families have different rules and ideas.' 'Our bodies are very sensitive and clever.' 'Not everybody follows the rules, and we can learn to be patient with them.'

My advice? Try everything! Sometimes, we've been pretending we're okay for so long, that we don't think we need or even deserve supports. Chances are, if you've been hearing autistics rave about something that helps, it's probably true for you, too! I remember thinking fidgets were just toys, until I held one! And weighted blankets? Gamechangers!

---

* Our brains tend to like rules, so think of these phrases as helping us shape our thinking. They are flexible 'rules' that help us understand and accept change.

Recovery and energy

Every autistic is different. But we all respond to our environment. We are sensitive to energy: sensory, social, and emotional. We pick up on patterns, probability, and personalities. While it can sometimes appear as though we react or change 'out of the blue', I promise you the build-up is long and the signs are everywhere.

Autistics are not 'oversensitive drama queens', 'cry baby attention seekers', or any of the other things we are so often called. Autistics experience energy as a kind of human mercury, responding and reacting to our environment. Time spent in the neurotypical world throws us out of balance. We hold ourselves together as well as we can, but even on what looks like a 'good' day, we can be worn down internally. When we are dysregulated, we need adequate rest and recovery time in a safe space. Here are some ideas for sensory recovery at home:

- **Downtime:** For example, time that is people-free, demand-free, etc.
- **Darkness:** For example, bed, tent, hut, egg chair, hammock, enclosed space.
- **Quiet:** For example, a quiet space or bedroom, or a controlled sound such as white noise, favourite music, favourite videos.
- **Textures, smells, visuals:** Objects to squeeze, squish, sniff, cuddle, watch, grip, chew, touch.

You can combine elements: soft coloured lights with falling glitter, hot baths with nice-smelling oils, a sensory swing, weighted vests or blankets, or maybe a little of everything! Ideas for sensory recovery can be as diverse as the sensory world, and the best part? Many of them can be easily incorporated into everyday life. Little things add up. You can layer sensory jewels into your life. A fidget here, a soft light there, and yes, these things might seem insignificant, but in the same way rain can feed a garden, you can make long-term change drop by drop.

The delicate balance of our senses and environment affects our wellbeing in every moment, and we can develop ways to understand, preserve, and replenish our energy.

Preserving energy

Autistics spend energy in ways that neurotypicals don't. We anticipate, notice, worry, feel, and stress differently from our neurotypical counterparts, and that's before we even get out of bed in the morning. So, we need to find ways to save energy in other areas of everyday life. For example:

- Use systems like online shopping, calendars, schedules, GPS for directions, etc.
- Simplify and pre-prepare. For example, repeating favourite meals, clothing, food, bag, etc.
- Consider minimizing your belongings (unless your autistic joy is collecting!).

Preserving energy can sometimes be one of the reasons autistics acquiesce to demands. We sometimes find that the conflict, the debate, the fight uses just too much energy. So, it might appear to others as though we don't care or don't understand things, when actually we are prioritizing what we can afford to spend energy on.

Consider all the decisions that need to be made each day,

and the regular, repeated tasks; look for areas that you can simplify, delegate, outsource, or automate.

Do you know the Spoon Theory? Developed by Christine Miserandino in 2003,[4] the Spoon Theory describes how people with chronic pain have to allocate their energy. The theory (technically an analogy) has been embraced by the autistic community as a way to explain how daily demands are met (or not). We all have a certain amount of energy to allocate each day. Different tasks, situations, and environments require different amounts of energy (spoons).

For me, I might have enough spoons to leave the house and make it to work, but not enough to talk while I'm there or do anything once I get home but sleep. This is why during my biggest shutdown, I could still get myself to the two physical commitments I had each week (classes and book club) and no one there would have known (or probably believed) that I got out of bed to be there, and went straight back to bed afterwards.

Everything requires spoons: getting dressed, having a shower, eating, making choices, office politics, social navigation, masking, the outside world. You may hear people say things like, 'I don't have the spoons for that' or, 'I'm out of spoons today.'

Efficient use of spoons is one explanation for common autistic traits: wearing the same clothing, eating the same foods, maintaining routine, etc. It's all about preserving energy and easing decision fatigue.

Decision fatigue

How many decisions do you think you make in a day? The average amount of remotely conscious decisions an adult makes each day is about thirty-five thousand. In contrast, young children only make about three thousand decisions each day.[5]

Decision fatigue is the idea that the more decisions you have to make, the less mental energy you have to make them. There are even studies proving that making decisions can weaken you physically. This means, the fewer trivial decisions you have to make in a day, the more energy and power you have to make the decisions that count (or, you know, live your life).

This could be one reason why so many autistic (and super-successful!) people use a capsule wardrobe, what we'd call 'wearing the same thing every day'. Famous examples include Barack Obama, Facebook's Mark Zuckerberg, Apple's Steve Jobs, and Anna Wintour from *Vogue*. Same basic wardrobe items. A heap of daily decisions pre-made.

Another way people do this is with the food they eat (researchers at Cornell found that people make an average of more than two hundred decisions – 226.7 to be exact – about food alone) – it's all about developing routines and conserving energy.[6]

Replenishing energy

Autistics can restore and recharge by spending time in special places. And not just where we live. Consider places away from home: the library? A grandparent's home? A corner of the classroom? And consider creating places at home: a hut in the lounge? A sensory corner? A bedroom?

Supporting autistics to find and explore what feels good to us will unlock tools for both peace and power. Let us know that it's okay to try things and that knowing what we don't want is as valuable as knowing what we do. Tell us that you know life can be hard for us in ways that others don't always understand, but that every little discovery is a win. The idea is to help us find what we love and fill our lives with it! It might be as simple as a colour, or as complex as an occupation, but finding ways to bring it into our lives will fill us with joy and replenish our energy.

Autistics are known for having specialties (often patronizingly referred to as 'special interests'. Um, how come neurotypicals just get to have 'passions' but we have 'special interests'?). These specialties can be innate (something you're born with) or acquired (something you develop), but the results of letting us immerse ourselves in them are always outstanding!

Other possible ways to recharge precious energy? Music, movies, books, TV shows, objects, toys, pets, writing, building, languages, swimming, swinging, insects, vehicles, sparkly things, squishy things, soft things, cooking, gaming, running, art, robotics, sewing, creating... Did you notice the stims in there?

Stim: short for 'self-stimulation'. A stim is a movement or sensation that is repeated to relieve stress. Autistics also stim because it feels good! Stims can be physical, auditory, visual, tactile. Stimming brings autistic joy!

Autistic joy

The autistic experience is life in high-def. Cranked-up sound, bright lights, intense colour – our brains and hearts on fire. When our senses work against us, the world is scary, hard, and demanding. But when our senses line up? When our interests are fed? When the elements inside and outside of us dance? Genius. Magic. Autistic joy.

Autistic joy is felt and expressed across all senses, activities, and environments. Autistics can experience joy through stimming (either automatically or on purpose), we buzz, we burn, we light up, we are utterly present. From the outside, we might look calm and peaceful, maybe zoned out, or we may be spinning and flapping, it all depends on how and what we are experiencing. Essentially, if meditation is the feeling of being 'at one with the universe', autistic joy is the feeling of being at one with the moment.

So, imagine that autistic joy does not describe a feeling, as much as a *way* of feeling, an intensity. A flow that runs through an activity, idea, or process. We find patterns, see connections, we love metaphor and analogies. We can get hyper-focused, fall in love, and become immersed in an attention tunnel. Suddenly, we're not just looking at something, we're feeling it, sensing it, we're connecting it with a million other things in our head. Throw in a fully absorbed sensory system, and can you imagine the shock of being yanked out of this state with a 'Hurry up!', 'It's time to go!', or 'Stop being silly.'

Just because you don't understand something, it doesn't make it invalid. Autistics sense and experience the world differently, and that often means connecting with nature, objects, or the non-human. We are the ones who will trace outlines, hug rocks, collect leaves. We will line up felt-tips in rainbow order and listen to the same song over and over. We will sense the mood of a day, reflect, and repeat what's around us. Like human mercury, right?

(If the gifts of autism include focused attention and being in the moment, our kryptonite is definitely change.)

Transitions

The Greek philosopher Heraclitus said: 'We both step and do not step in the same rivers. We are and are not.' Moment to moment, our environment changes, we change. Transitions can be minor, major, daily, irregular, and for many human beings, plain as oxygen, barely noticeable. But for neurodivergent brains? Transitions expose us to one of our greatest stresses: the unknown. Life is made up of transitions, movement between activities or environments; and for neurodivergent brains, transitions take on a different intensity.

We don't have the luxury of numbness, blunt nerve endings, or the option of developing a 'we'll cross that bridge when we come to it' attitude. We are wired to feel stress at change. Ideally, a good transition is no transition, but in a world where 'Change is the only constant' (Heraclitus again), autistics and our navigators can benefit from paying special attention to transitions of all kinds.

Here's the goal: to create smooth, gradual, and more positive transitions. And we are not only sensitive to environmental transitions, but to social and emotional changes, expectations, logistics, and our own physical and emotional states. (Oh cool, is that all? #Sarcasm.) For example, some autistics register the transition between concrete and grass as completely different tactile sensations, a jolt to the system. Other autistics react strongly to a subtle change in temperature, different packaging, or someone else's haircut. All these little changes affect us. They also build up.

Think about the bedtime routines we have for babies: A bath with special smells, lavender oil massage and a song, gentle teeth brushing, into bed with a soothing story, soft lighting, warm room... We send small humans as many sensory signals as we can to transition to sleep. Why? Because we are desperate for them to sleep! We throw every tool we have at transitioning babies to sleep because it is our priority! We don't know exactly what works, so we try everything. As time goes on, we take transitions, like going from awake to asleep, for granted. But what if we didn't?

What if we prioritized smooth transitions? Not necessarily as full-on as the sleep routine for a baby, but certainly that consistent. Predictable routine, repeated meals, transition songs, certain words or phrases, stories. Positive sensory triggers built into your world. The more comfort and expectation we can put around transitions, the easier they will be for autistics of every age and magic.

It's only since my diagnosis that I've realized how much I have implemented over time to soothe (or smother) my own anxiety, especially around transitions and change. I make myself detailed schedules, maps, and plans. I research. I practise meditation. I watch the same movies over and over. I have my favourite foods, routes, ways of doing things. It's all about doing as much as possible to build scaffolding around new events and routine around existing ones.

For me, changes in routine are like that awesome feeling when someone cancels plans you didn't really want to have in the first place. Suddenly, your whole day just opens up, suddenly clear and free; maybe you won't even put on pants. Transitions can feel like the *opposite* of that. This is going to your favourite restaurant for breakfast expecting a bagel and they've just kicked off the daytime menu. Now you have to re-jig your tongue and your brain, *and your day*, because you were fully expecting a bagel and now you have to process a burger.

I'm an adult, but even I resist transitioning tricks that I know are for my own good. It's my internalized ableism. I just hate the idea of feeling less-than or spoiled, but I try to tell myself this isn't pandering or babying, this is being respectful of neurological differences.

Change is the only constant. And autistics can need to be gently reminded of that so we can use our energy to prepare rather than resist. Different transitions and different people will benefit from different strategies, but here are some ideas:

- **Involve us in transitions:** Be open and honest, matter of fact, identify the challenges together, respect and acknowledge our point of view. Remember that your job isn't to debate whether anticipated hopes or fears will be realized, but to acknowledge that potential outcomes are possible, and stressful, whether they are realized or not.
- **Create a profile of the autistic person's key information:** Their interests, passions, preferences, needs, challenges. Identify any existing strategies and consider ways to put them in place.
- **Make the unknown known:** Arrange regular visits to a new location before the actual transition happens,

with no rush, and no agenda. Aim for familiarization, building relationships, alleviating anxiety. This can be done in person or online, whatever is available and works best for everyone involved.

- **Create visuals:** Maps, photos, pictures, schedules, routines. Use a diary or planner, colour-coded checklists, countdowns.
- **Can you connect with any humans who could help?** People (peers, buddies, mentors, etc.) can help provide navigation, orientation, or the comfort of experience and prior knowledge.
- **Create a safe space:** Can you make a safe space or person available? A place to provide continuity and familiarity, a place to find calm and switch off or vent if necessary.

Remember, this is not about dealing with one event. We are looking for ways to support and empower autistics to handle transitions and change over our lifetime, not just one particular situation. For example:

- **Growing up:** Read books about growing up and answer any questions openly. Find role-models and examples of autistics growing up, finding their strengths and succeeding.
- **Uncovering passions, strengths, and skills:** There are so many options; look for the ones that feel good and blend with existing passions and skills.

Consider strategies together. Getting buy-in is important.

Show the autistic that there can be flexibility, but that the most important thing is their happiness and comfort, and that your priority is supporting them. The autistic is the centre of their world; empower them to know that.

Here's another idea that may help. In construction, a *specified tolerance* is the amount that a measurement can vary and still be considered accurate. An allowable variation. This idea can be useful for autistics as it allows us to practise some flexibility, but also provides guidance within a rule. For example, 'We'll go shoe shopping for one hour. At a minimum, we'll look at the shoes and get an idea of what's available. And if you're feeling good, and things are going well, maximum tolerance, we'll try some shoes on and buy a pair you like. But if we just get to the shop and have a look, that will be enough for today.'

Important: This is not the time to pull a bait-and-switch, don't give us a minimum to trick us into the maximum. If you tell us the minimum is to look in the shop, that has to be enough for you. Interestingly enough, if you don't push a demand, an autistic is more likely to feel comfortable and suggest it themselves. It's not reverse psychology, you're not being clever or sneaky, you're just giving the autistic the freedom and space to make the most comfortable and logical choice themselves. Many of us have a Pervasive Desire for Autonomy. Go with it!

After-school strategies

Start from a place of appreciation for your child – they made it! A school day is often long, hard, stressful, and exhausting. We cannot imagine the battles and challenges our children face. So, keep the expectations low. From their point of view, it is huge that they survived the day. Truly. So, in your mind, stay present and be grateful. Appreciate that this is the end of a big day. The transition after school is a reset. Keep the atmosphere quiet and low-demand. Plan to get to their comfort/joy/special interest as smoothly and easily as possible. Have a routine that follows their after-school needs. For example:

- **Toilet:** A child may have been holding – or unable to go – all day. This could be more than being forgetful or distracted, it could be due to sensitivities. Going to the bathroom is a physical task that can be affected by mental and emotional stress. Do not underestimate the sensory and social challenges of the school toilets. This is not about logic, this is a physical reaction to the environment. You may be able to talk to them about it, but you probably can't change the physical facilities. If the first thing your child needs when they get home is the toilet? Don't make a big deal out of it, and don't chastise them for trusting their body.
- **Food:** If your child eats very little at school, it probably has nothing to do with the food itself and everything to do with the environment. For autistics, eating away from a safe place can be difficult and sometimes impossible. It could be due to anxiety, sensory and social overwhelm, or stress.

But whatever is going on, the energy needs of survival in the moment can outweigh the need (or even desire) to eat. So, our body allocates energy accordingly. For example, if you had to eat during a panel job interview? Even your favourite food would probably taste like mattress-stuffing, and that's if you could focus enough to get it in your mouth. Eating food, processing food, enjoying food, requires energy. The kind of energy autistics are often using to scan for hazards, control their expressions, process mistakes, filter words, analyse the people around them, anticipate reactions, hold in stims, and brace for what's looming. (Yes, even children, and yes, even if you think we can be 'ourselves' around you.)

Food can be many things, a joy, a challenge, a tool, a toy, an obstacle, a pathway, but one consistency? Food is relentless. It is many meals, every day, so you need to decide: Do you want to take this on as a permanent, ongoing, years-long struggle? Or do you want to figure out what works for your child? Your love and validation will mean more to them than regular lunches (I promise). Open your mind, there is always a way! Does your child enjoy a big breakfast? Could they eat a main meal in the morning and a smaller 'safe food' at school for lunch? Or are they super-hungry when they get home? Could they/the family have dinner then? Meal times, like so much of our current world, are antiquated customs we've dragged along with us through time. Maybe it's time to consider new ways that work for us now?

- **Clothing:** Autistics prioritize comfort and consistency wherever possible. This means we can be super-sensitive about what we wear. Having comfy 'home clothes' to change into can be a smart way both to transition from school and to ensure washing opportunities for favourite clothing. Wearing clothes that feel wrong to your body all day is exhausting. Let home be our safe place in all ways.
- **Lighting and temperature:** Your child may like all the curtains in their rooms closed. They may like to be under a blanket and next to the fire. It may not feel right for you, but it is what their body needs to regulate. If you're not quite ready to change the whole house, can you let their room be a space under their control?

Warning: Immediately after school is not the time to grill them about their day. Answering questions can be exhausting (especially when you're trying to figure out the right thing to say, not hurt a parent's feelings, etc.). Don't make them responsible for making you feel better about their day.

Once your child has food, comfort, relaxation, and they have transitioned to their safe home space, you may like to ask a couple of questions. Here are some question tips:

- **Keep your tone light and casual:** Ideally? Find a way to be present and available but mildly distracted. For example, ask while you are preparing food, lightly cleaning or organizing, or building some Lego®. That way, it's less like a forced interrogation, and more like an optional invitation. A subtle but important difference, I promise.

Have you heard of parallel play? It's when two people enjoy separate activities alongside each other. Parallel play is used to describe a type of toddler play, but actually nails one of the ways autistics enjoy communicating. For example, both people reading, but different books. Everyone watching a movie, while gaming on their own devices. If you are with us, we know, and your pure presence is enough. Comfortably sharing space while absorbed in our own interest.

- **Ensure questions are simple and specific:** What did you learn in maths? What was the funniest thing that happened at school today? (Be conscious of your objective here, what is it you are really asking? Autistics have a knack for sensing the intention behind a question. So, ask about their day if you are interested, but if what you really want to know is 'Are you happy at school?' you probably already know the answer and want them to make you feel better. Don't ask any question to which you can't handle a truthful answer.
- **Questions can often work best at the end of the day, in bed, dark, quiet, safe:** Create a low-pressure, high-trust space. Let them know that you will not overreact or be upset with anything

they share (only promise if you can either keep the promise or know you have the humility to apologize sincerely if you break it).

Communication

We need to stop the parents and professionals looking for a cure. Looking to change who we are. Instead? We need them to learn our language and communication style. We need to let the parents know that they are enough, more than enough, that they can trust their hearts and listen to their kids. Because whether an autistic uses words, actions, sign language, or any other of a thousand communication signals: We know what we want and don't want. We know who respects us. We know who we love. Our instincts are not only strong, but they are unfettered by the 'shoulds' and 'musts' of the neurotypical world. And guess what? Now we have the research to back it up!

Autistic researcher Dr Damian Milton, who developed the 'double empathy theory', writes: 'Individuals who have different ways of processing and experiencing the world will also have differing norms and expectations and would therefore find it difficult to empathise with each other.'[7]

'Double empathy' says that a mismatch between two people can lead to faulty communication. This means it is easier for people with similar neurotypes to communicate with each other. What would it look like if, instead of training our autistics to be more like neurotypicals (Quiet hands! Make eye contact! Be more social! Sit still! Suck it up! Pretend!), we started training neurotypicals to be more like autistics?

(Tell the truth! Be direct! Fidget! Stim! Read upside down! Scream if you need to!)

Have you seen autistic children together? Suddenly, the same children who are 'disruptive' in their classroom or 'outsiders' in their school, are calm, productive members of a group. It's an unspoken sense of belonging, of being with people who 'get you' – the security of like-minds. Research continues to prove what neurodivergents already know: We have our own ways of doing things, and our ways are not wrong – they are just not (yet!) recognized as acceptable or valid. Autistics socialize more effectively with other autistics. For us, communicating with neurotypicals is like a foreign language. Research based on the telephone game has shown that groups of autistics communicate effectively with each other, groups of neurotypicals communicate effectively with each other – it is only communication in groups that include both autistics and neurotypicals that is compromised.[8] So, here's a quick guide to autistic vs. neurotypical communication:

Communication	Neurodivergent	Neurotypical
Words and meaning	Direct, blunt	Indirect, white lies
Silence	Comfortable	Uncomfortable
Conversation style	Info-dumping, monologuing	Small talk, dialoguing
Show listening and interest	Through whole body listening and remembering	Through eye contact and immediate response
Empathy shown	Through sharing similar experiences	Through verbal reinforcements

What if we stopped asking people to be verbal, to communicate the way we want them to? Who says eye contact makes you a good communicator? Why do we consider verbal ability a measure of success? A measure of anything? What if we decided to become better receivers? Try it. Don't use words for a day. Obviously, this is nothing like situational mutism, but it will open your mind.

Notice how you now express your wants and feelings, your love, notice how seldom people's words match their intention. How much more you can understand without the pressure of creating, weighing, and ejecting words through sound.

If you're not autistic, not neurodivergent, you get to choose. So, choose to be open to a new world, a world where normal is old-school and the status quo is the first thing to go! Choose to learn our communication style, because we have no choice about learning yours.

Thank you for being here, for listening. That desire, that willingness, means more than any one strategy. That you see us, and respect us, because of (not in spite of) our differences. Let's move from strategies that allow for survival and move towards creating a world where we can all feel safe and welcome. Inclusion is no longer about writing policies or ticking boxes, but about wrapping us up in a world that works for everyone.

Expectations

Changing the world for autistics ultimately makes the world better for everyone. And it starts by letting go of expectations. Start now! Let go of what you have been told, and what you believe, life is supposed to look like. Choose happy over 'normal'. Take nothing for granted! What do I mean?

- **Success:** How do you define success? Money? Love? Peace? Friends? For example: What do you want for your children? (And is it really for them?) Do you want them to have friends because you think that makes them happy? When maybe delicious new books and alone time are what really makes them happy. And that's okay. Success, happiness, the 'real' world is what we decide and create. Don't be uber-qualified and unhappy, don't be the best at a job you don't love, don't be rolling in money but alone. Decide what success and happiness means for you, then dismantle any belief that gets in the way of what works for you.
- **Touch:** Don't assume that because touch is comforting to you, it will be to others. Non-touchy autistics may not show love physically the same way you do, or want, or expect. They're probably never going to run up to you and smother you with hugs and kisses. That's not who they are. Do you want them to pretend? For you? Or can you love them enough to accept the ways they do show love?
- **Showing love:** Physical touch is one way to show love, verbal expressions are another, but there are so many more. Connect through learning together, or truly seeing someone. Show love by letting someone be, by sharing space and silence. Notice how the autistic in your life connects with you, maybe by

checking on you with eyes or fingertips, by sharing memes, by being themselves. By being true.

- **Offices:** Why not consider flexible, work-from-home options? Light dimmers, headphones, new ways of working together and connecting?
- **Photographs:** Do we have to have a traditional family photo? If the photoshoot is stressful, the clothes itchy, and the facials forced, what memories are you actually creating? How can we capture memories of our family in ways that feel good to all of us?
- **Learning:** Do students have to sit still while they learn? Does every individual in a class have to work on the same projects, at the same level, at the same time? Do assessments need to be written?
- **Teaching:** Imagine lifting the burden on teachers, allowing them to be guides and facilitators. As much neuro navigators as leaders and instructors. What would happen if teachers became a safe space, a 'soft place to fall'? What a difference this could make? Especially when students may not feel comfortable sharing their diagnosis, their needs, their identity. They may not even be aware of it.
- **School:** Many autistics describe their education experience as 'I loved to learn, the problem with school was everything else.' How could we change the school environment to support neurodivergent learners and educators?
- **Parenting:** What if we didn't have to know everything? What if we let our children lead us?

Could we set our ego aside, and accept that we are all here to learn and grow together?

- **Holidays:** Does a holiday have to mean leaving the country, or the house? Is it really a break if you are more stressed than hanging out together at home?
- **Food:** Do we have to eat at the dinner table? If the autistic is happier eating alone, in their room, at the coffee table, out of a paper bag, does it really matter? Maybe our family moments don't happen at meal times, maybe they happen on long drives, exploring nature, or lying on the floor. What does being a family look like for us?

Consider all the different areas or activities in your family, your home, or organization. Look at them from a sensory point of view, an autistic point of view. Are there changes you could make? Different things you could try? Let's stop spending energy or enforcing rules to support a cookie-cutter, holiday-card world that isn't real. What if you stopped caring what the world thinks, and start changing how it feels?

Food

The first time I met autistic kids, what struck me was that they eat like me, or rather, like the me that eats when no one is watching. Food carefully selected (no, all the hot chips are not the same, I want that. Specific. Slithery. One), separated on the plate, in the right order, in the right shape, then meticulously picked apart for the right texture and to eliminate surprises. It's like the food is talking, giving off energy. It's like autistics can see, feel, hear, and sense things about the food that neurotypical brains can't.

Okay, so what's the deal? Why do autistics generally have such a limited diet? Why the plain pasta? Why all the processed food? Why the nuggets? So many reasons: sensory, comfort, colours, textures, tastes, smells, allergies, intolerances... Nutrition can often be at the bottom of the priority heap. As an adult, I have a far more extensive palate than I did as a kid, but I still have specific things I eat, and places I'll go, things I order. Don't get me wrong, I can be flexible (with at least seven days' notice #Haha). But I do have very specific brands and processes for eating. Nothing my parents did or didn't do could have changed that. It's just that, as an adult, I have the luxury of being in charge of my own food. I didn't grow out of my food weirdness, I grew into it.

When your child is neurodivergent, food challenges are not bad parenting, and it's not just this one kid. Something is going on here, with our kids, our brains, our food, something that's bigger than all of us. And yay for the internet, because we used to be alone with our worries, but now we can find hundreds of other parents who are wrapping homemade nuggets in takeaway wrappers to try and get some semblance of a nutrient into their autistic kid.

I get it, I'm on the same planet, with lectures on the food pyramid, emphasis on healthy eating, posters celebrating vegetables. Meanwhile, your kid is eating the same three things and that's it. They like it very certain ways – the shapes, colours, textures, the environment around eating has to be exactly right. For a parent, it is exhausting; but for an autistic, it is life and death. Well, not literally life and death, but remember how much of the world is out of your control when you're a kid; things like repetition, ritual, food, become lifelines, ways to hold yourself together when the world makes no sense. And yes, we'll try new things, maybe even like them, but the process needs to be gentle and respectful.

Your autistic kid can probably scale six-foot fences and run like the wind, they may have no fear of traffic, be able to stay up all night bouncing off the walls, so let's agree: they are (probably*) not going to get scurvy and fade away. Our kids are clever and strong, their brains and bodies are magical. Honestly, they could probably eat Play-Doh-dirt martinis and be sweet-as. You are doing your best and they are going to be okay. So, what would happen if we trusted these sensitivities, instead of fighting them?

If you're searching how to sneak vegetables into cake, it's because you love your kid. You're coming from that place where great parenting is vegetables, manners, and boundaries. Things are changing fast. Our kids are processing ideas and feelings in different ways. The human body is a delicate machine, and I promise you, we feel your disappointment, your stress, and anxiety around meal times. We know you want us to smile and pretend, to force down the foods you give us. But for us it means going against every signal our body is sending. Please don't make us choose between pleasing you

* Disclaimer: I'm not a nutritionist, if you're worried about nutrition, go to a doctor. You know your body, your child, so if you get a funny feeling, get it checked out. But once you are confident that food issues are something other than nutrients and proteins, blood tests and food pyramid and blah, blah, blah, come back here.

and trusting our body. Consider that the love you give your child, the presence, the acceptance, will light up their DNA faster than broccoli and stronger than spinach. Consider that the energy in your family around food, your relationships, your role-modelling, your attitude and environment, is going to make more of a difference to your kid's health and wellbeing than whether they're eating pancakes five times a day for a month #TrueStory.

For neuro navigators, the food fight is an energy exchange. It's decisions about how much energy you have, and how you want to best spend that energy. Do you have the energy to cut the sandwiches into an unsolvable puzzle? To build towers and faces out of vegetables? Do you have the energy to engage your child in the gardening, prepping, and cooking process, to make the food safe and familiar for them? Can you consider any movement towards different food experiences a win? Because for autistics, smelling something new is huge. Touching it, considering it. This is why involving kids in growing, preparing, and cooking food can be helpful. This time and intent creates chemical changes that can make all the difference. In the human and the food. But it also could be a whole lot of effort and you still end up cooking nuggets for dinner. (No judgement here, yay nuggets!) In the end, if you have the energy, try all the things. If it's fun for you, if it's play for your kid, if you can laugh when you spend an hour prepping and they won't even touch it because it doesn't 'look right', dooo it!

But don't let it break your heart, don't make food another thing you beat yourself up about, another way you think you're failing as a parent. Food is every day, for ever. This cannot be about getting through the day, because sometimes it's all you can do to get through a morning. Instead, spend your energy on your relationship, the feeling in your family, because that will build them up more surely than the perfect food pyramid. Stop freaking out about what's going in their mouth and focus on what's going in their heart.

Role-modelling is the most powerful tool you have. But again, you only have so much energy to put on the show. If the food fight is becoming bigger than your relationship, drop it. Offer the green things, but don't trick, demand, or force. Autistics need to be free to make good choices from the inside, not to please you or anyone else. (And isn't that what we want for them as grown-up humans anyway?)

You can create traditions around food, let them be part of the growing, preparing, and cooking process so much that eating it becomes totally matter of fact. You can talk about doing tough things first, delayed gratification, all the amazingness and nutrients of dirt animals, do all that, but let their bodies be their choice. Your love is unconditional, right? Obviously, you don't love them less if they only eat nuggets. But maybe you sigh, you frown, you give them a million little signs that you disapprove. And maybe it's the food you disapprove of, but to a child it is them. Ooh, and while we're here: your language. When you say a child is 'picky and difficult,' you make it sound like we have a choice. We don't. Our body is throwing a million different signals at us, urging us to follow. But when you say, 'picky and difficult,' do you know what your child hears? *Too hard. Too much. A problem. A burden.* All your child truly wants (I promise) is to say yes, to be easy, and to make you happy. Imagine the courage it takes to resist adults, every meal, every day, to go against the people in their life they love the most. To trust their body, to trust their heart.

Your child is not being 'difficult', they are desperate for peace and safety, internal and external. And actually? Your child is *selective*, they are *super-sensitive*, they're figuring out their clever bodies by listening, trusting the signals. Help them by being on their side.

And I'm not saying let them swim in a chocolate fountain, I'm just saying be a team and work together. Never get into a battle of wills with an autistic. Not only because you'll never ever win. But because you and your child are not adversaries, you're *whānau*, family. You are on team Your Kid, and it's you guys against a world that already makes their life pretty bloody hard. Be their soft place to fall, and that doesn't mean give them everything they want, it means love them no matter what, and keep food – something you will do together every day, over and over and over again – from being another stress on your family. (Actually, scratch that. If you ever have the opportunity to swim in a chocolate fountain, take it!)

Obviously, I'm one autistic. As you'll know by now, we're all from the same planet, but we're all different. If you have an autistic in your life, let them explain their preferences. Your job will be to act like the cool, calm, and totally accepting parent or professional that you know you are. Different things work for different people, and remember that we are playing the long game here. We're raising kids in a world where compliance and conformity is not just boring but dangerous. I want my kids to say no, to speak their truth and stand up for themselves, and (sometimes frustratingly) that means I have to honour their truth if they think the broccoli is trying to kill them. But maybe frozen peas are an acceptable alternative.

Being autistic is like being gluten intolerant: you can get rid of the gluten at home, but not in the world. Over time, you alter your life to avoid and minimize your triggers. So, it can look like autistic adults are 'less autistic' have 'grown out of it' or are 'functioning well', when actually we just have strategies in place. These strategies can be as deliberate as choosing clothes without seams, or as accidental as feeling drawn to work in a library. So much of the stress and anxiety of neurodivergence is hating yourself for not coping. But tools and strategies empower autistics to accept our wiring.

You may live with autistics, work with us, or only come across an autistic person once in your life, but you have the power to make that encounter life-changing. Not because you say the *perfect* thing or do the *perfect* thing, but because like every individual, your values, the way you see the world, your attitude, and the way you work and approach people, ripples out into the world.

Breaking Point

So, we've seen the complex kaleidoscope of autistic traits, strengths, challenges, and sensitivities. Being super-sensitive can be a lot. So, what happens when an autistic is overwhelmed? Shutdown. Meltdown. Burnout.

Shutdown

Like sneezing or smiling, a shutdown is the physical expression, it's the breaking point after a build-up. A shutdown can happen suddenly or build up over time. It can last a few moments or months at a time.

A shutdown can look like:	A shutdown can feel like:
Glazed eyes	Heavy body
Physical stillness	Numb heart
Withdrawing, disappearing, or isolating	Blank brain
Sleeping or lying down	A crushing weight

cont.

A shutdown can look like:	A shutdown can feel like:
Going quiet	A black hole
Hiding	Being invisible

If someone you love is autistic, a shutdown is their cocoon, their cast, their insulin. Shutdown is not for ever, it's not your fault, and the best thing you can do is truly, respectfully support them.

- Provide what they need: darkness, isolation, pillows, weighted blankets.
- Tell them it's okay (and mean it).
- Remove as many commitments and obligations from them as you can.
- Tuck them in (if they like that) and tell them it will take as long as it takes. Everything is okay, and you are there for them.
- Be Teflon™. This is not personal. They are not being manipulative, lazy, or stubborn. Remember this is an uncontrollable physical reaction. This is your child at breaking point. They are physically broken and need time to heal. Shutdown is chicken pox without the dots, and just as deserving of love and sympathy.

They probably feel frustrated, useless, and weak. Tell them that taking care of themselves is the best thing they can do (and mean it), tell them that it will be okay. Because it really will be okay. Your job is to support them, to put strategies in place so shutdown can be the totally regular and understandable part of autistic life that it truly is.

Meltdown

The same way that a shutdown is an involuntary physical reaction to stress, meltdowns are a temporary loss of control.

A meltdown can look like:	A meltdown can feel like:
Crying	Disconnected body
Screaming	Desperate brain
Being unable to speak	Fearful heart
Kicking	
Loss of physical control	
Running	Loss of emotional control
Hiding	Overwhelming stress and anxiety

An autistic meltdown is a feeling of being completely out of control, a physical build-up of stress, and it can happen in a split second or build up over time.

A meltdown is a physical reaction. It can be due to: stress, sensory overload, frustration, injury or pain, communication difficulties, lack of sleep, hurt or neglect, an overwhelmed brain, not knowing what they need or how to express it, a request for connection.

A meltdown is a physical reaction. It is not due to: bad parenting, attention seeking, being spoiled, being selfish, lack of discipline, enjoying the behaviour, lack of self-control, manipulating people, throwing a tantrum, lack of respect. Again, a meltdown is breaking point. It is as valid as a broken bone.

Your best tool (and sometimes the toughest!) is going to be role-modelling, showing the autistic in your life what calm looks, sounds, and feels like – keeping yourself calm, acting like you have all the time in the world, even when you don't (especially then). It's all about the kind eyes, truly being present, and open-minded. Be the calm in the storm until they find themselves.

Burnout

Burnout is intense exhaustion. It can be physical, mental, and/or emotional, and is a consequence of long-term masking. Burnout is what happens when an autistic 'fakes normal' for long periods by suppressing autistic traits without downtime or recovery. The autistic has been doing too much, being too much, pretending too much, and the brain pulls rank on the body. Burnout is what happens when an autistic's operating system gives out.

Burnout can look like:	Burnout can feel like:
Loss of function	Overwhelm
Loss of self-care skills	Exhaustion
Isolation	Social overload
Low energy	Inability to maintain neurotypical mask
Resistance to making decisions	Being empty
Easily triggered into overload	Being unplugged from power
Regression	Guilt, shame, and depression

On top of expending energy blending into the regular world,

many autistics have their support needs questioned. This is because as they learn to appear more neurotypical, their challenges are even less recognized by those around them, so they end up having to pretend even more. The bar is raised higher and higher to an exhausting (and impossible) standard. Can you love us even when we are too tired to put on the show for you?

Regulated autistics are not broken, and do not need to be fixed. Being autistic is who and how we are. What we need is support through the overwhelm and strategies to ease life as much as possible.

Self-care for autistics

My body is so used to living in a state of anxiety that it doesn't register stress chemicals, so they build up. This often keeps me on the edge of overload and burnout. This is also why it looks like I'm going off because you touched my pen, when actually you touching my pen is just the tipping point after a build-up of days or months or years of a string of little stresses and challenges.

My doctor said that because of the way I sense things and process things, my life is harder. I have to remind myself about that. Because it's not babying me; it's just a fact. I'm playing the game of life in hard mode. It's why the average lifespan of autistics is so much shorter than their neurotypical peers, and why one of the leading causes of death in our culture is suicide. I don't feel sad about that, and it's not because I don't have feelings (haha #AutismMyth). I just get it. When everywhere you look is big and hard, when you don't belong, when life is dark, why wouldn't death be a relief? Just because I don't have or express feelings like the majority, it doesn't mean I don't have feelings. I cry watching movies, reading books, even over sad advertisements and songs, because to me, they are sad. But divorce to me is not sad. Real-life people grow up, grow apart, they're happier on their own. High-five and yay them. Who decides which feelings are normal or appropriate?

When someone breaks their leg, we don't say, 'Just walk it off!' We understand that in a single moment, we can cause damage that takes weeks to undo. Sure, walk on your broken leg. It'll still heal. It'll just take longer. Same with autistic overwhelm; an autistic can sometimes push through, use their desensitized brain to drag their body around and make it do their bidding, but there will be consequences. Physical, emotional, mental.

You can walk on your broken leg, push through, walk it off; but you will be broken for longer. The damage is done, and the healing process is lengthened. Self-care needs to be built into our lifestyle. Do not wait until breaking point to find the energy, space, and resources to look after yourself. Strategies aim to make your life better. If you've hit breaking point, you're too late. This time. But you have a lifetime ahead of you. Being sensitive is your gift and your burden, honour it with self-care.

First Steps

The time following diagnosis or someone sharing their identity with you can be a blur. Information overload, myths, statistics, opinions – all while riding on an emotional rollercoaster. Take a breath. Take your time. Here are some simple truths if you find out you are autistic, if you find out your friend or colleague is autistic, or if you find out your child is autistic.

If you find out you are autistic:

- **You are still the same person:** Now you just know more about how you process the world, and how to make your life better.
- **Be kind to yourself:** It's okay to be angry. It's okay to be sad, relieved, or anything else. You may start seeing your past differently and be reprocessing your entire life. Take your time.
- **You are in control:** You can decide to learn more, talk to people, research, and process your diagnosis however you want (as long as you are safe). Or you can decide to press pause, wait a while, give yourself some time and come back to it when you feel

ready. If you identify, how you identify (publicly and privately) is your choice. Whether you share your diagnosis, or any other information, is up to you.

- **The best part? You are not alone:** There is a community of autistic adults, across genders, ages, skills, and talents. All diverse, and all dealing with the same issues, and at different points of the same journey. You may not belong in your family, your workplace, or your community, but you belong in this world. We are all finding our way and by doing this, we build a new world for the autistics who follow us.

If you find out a friend, colleague, or acquaintance is autistic:

- **They are still the same person:** Don't let a label change the way you see them or treat them.
- **Don't assume:*** Don't assume that the autistic needs or wants support, pity, or your questions. Before you ask a question, check with yourself: Am I asking out of a desire to understand or simple curiosity?
- **Trust them:** Don't question their diagnosis. Don't diminish their challenges. Reaching out and being vulnerable takes courage. Honour that by believing them instantly and every time.

---

* Whatever you know, or think you know, about being autistic, may not apply to this particular autistic. Come from a respectful, humble, and open place. Even if you have an autistic friend, even if you did a course, read a book, or have a Master's in autism. You are not the expert here. Autistics are all very different, and very individual.

If you find out your child is autistic:

- **Your child is still the same person:** Now you just know more about how they experience the world, and how you can support them to thrive.
- **You are the best person to be their parent:** The way you love and see your child is everything. You are their champion and their safe place. Don't let your hesitation, fear, ego, or anything else be bigger than what's best for your child.
- **Trust your child:** It is real for them – if they say a sound is hurting them, or something makes them uncomfortable, believe them. They see and feel and hear the world differently.
- **A diagnosis is not a prediction:** We are learning more about autism all the time. What was is not what will be. The limitations are lies, and everything is possible!
- **The best part? You are not alone:** You are now part of an incredibly experienced and supportive community. When you're ready, find them.

We're all looking for belonging and appreciation, and we read it in the eyes of the people around us.

When you meet someone, when you interact with someone, do your eyes light up? Do they light up with delight, acceptance, love? So now you know, the autistic in your life (your friend, your child, you) has the kind of magical brain that is here to change the world and make us all kinder, braver, more sensitive people.

Check your heart

In the end, if you don't really get it, if you don't truly know and believe that autistics experience the world differently, then any other changes you make will be hollow.

Many autistics can feel or read the energy around them. Even the youngest of us detect patterns – like expressions, tone, repeated behaviour and body language. This means you can do all the right things, maybe even say all the right things – but if you are holding on to resentment, impatience, or anger, we can feel it.

Making changes to the environment for an autistic is meeting support needs and accessibility requirements. You are not babying us, spoiling us, or walking on eggshells, you are respecting our neurological differences, and meeting our needs.

Consider how you ooze energy:

- **Tell your face:** Consider your expressions. Do you roll your eyes during conversations? Narrow them? Many autistics find eye contact painful; this doesn't mean that we aren't acutely aware of what you are doing with your eyes. Relax your brow, soften your eyes, remember that this is a person that you love. Even when they're confusing or frustrating!
- **Tell your voice:** Do you raise your voice to make a point? Harden or tighten your tone? Grit your teeth when you're trying not to yell? Consider how you speak to an animal – soft voice, open heart, wide eyes. Listen to how your voice sounds, or might sound to someone else. It's being vulnerable and present – not patronizing.

- **Tell your body:** You take up physical space. You are a buzzing ball of energy. When you stand over someone, hands on hips, pointing or gesturing – you are intimidating, big, scary. Even if you don't mean to be. Remember that we are all on the same team. Sit softly, unfold your arms, be conscious of how you use the space around you. Autistics feel it. It all matters.

Many autistics do not express emotions on their face, or in ways that other people can easily read. This does not mean we don't feel emotions. If anything, research and anecdotal evidence suggests many autistics feel incredibly deeply, and sometimes have to block or shut out emotion that is too strong for us to handle. What does this mean? It means that you need to trust that your words are enough. You don't need to raise your voice, gesture angrily, or escalate in any way. We hear you. Even when it doesn't seem like it. So, before every communication, take a breath. Consider your intentions.

You

Here's the biggest tip: the one that will 100% definitely, for sure, more than anything else, make the biggest difference to everyone around you: It's you. Your attitude, your understanding. People who get it make the difference. With your open heart, soft non-judgey eyes, you're taking the time to slow down, understand, to ask questions, and to care. This is how you support autistics in your home and in the world.

Bonus: Remember to learn from autistics! Use your preferred media (books, audio, social media platforms, etc.) and search for #ActuallyAutistic – this will help you find content created by autistics. Like, subscribe, watch, listen, learn, and absorb! Every bit of learning makes a difference!

Putting it all together

We started with the kaleidoscope, the spectrum of sensitivities that combine to make autistics exactly who they are. We learned that autism has a wide range of traits and variables, but at its core is a different way of experiencing the world. We now know that a diagnosis is not a prediction – it doesn't determine what is possible for a person. It just gives them (and you!) the tools, strategies, and understanding to make the most of who they are.

You've learned about empowering language. You understand how the language has developed and how your words make a difference. You can check in with the words you use: Are they supportive and uplifting? Do they reflect your beliefs? We've looked at the different sensitivities and how they bring both everyday challenges and incredible magic. We explored ways you can support these sensitivities and maybe even join this beautiful world.

You've learned how to honour and protect energy. How to support autistics at breaking point.

You've found ways you can connect with people who 'get it', people on the same journey, with the same challenges and adventures. You are not alone. Far from it, you are part of a huge community of people who are strong, sensitive, and changing the world. Even when you feel sure you're broken, especially then. You are making a difference.

So, now what? You can continue reading, learning, researching autism – but know this: You already have all the tools you need. Your open heart, your respectful curiosity. Your optimism, and your kind eyes. You have the power to change how you see the world, and how you see autistics. Use it.

In the following sections I'll focus on three environments where neuro navigators can make the biggest difference. Spoiler alert: The common theme is respect. Respect for difference, respect for needs, and respect for each other as humans.

You'll notice I use the Social Model of Disability. This says that people are disabled by a world that is not set up to accommodate their differences. This means a person is disabled not because they use a wheelchair but because their workplace does not have wide enough door frames or walkways. Translate that to neurodivergencies: We are disabled by environments built for typical brains:

- Spaces that don't consider sensory sensitivity, that are too loud, bright, or overwhelming.
- Processes that require speedy processing skills (like face-to-face communication or phone calls) or high levels of executive function (like completing and juggling multiple application forms and appointment times).

Universal design* means spaces, products, and systems that can be used by people of different situations and abilities. Because do you know who benefits from wider walkways and self-opening doors? People carrying things. People with prams. People with dyspraxia, crutches, walkers, and, oh yeah, wheelchair users. Human needs are universal, and acknowledging our needs is empowering. Universal design means putting people first, all people. It means believing that we can make the world better with spaces that work for every kind of human. For example, what happens when classrooms allow headphones, sensory and movement breaks, what happens when the transition to tertiary includes clear support, maps, apps, mentoring, options?

Disability does not describe a person, it expresses support requirements to navigate the current world. In a fully accessible world, not only is there no disability, but all people thrive. Let's add to this that being able-bodied is temporary. Over the course of a human lifetime, we all experience support needs – from reading glasses to pregnancy – and mobility challenges, even a broken finger will suddenly show you the value of recorded lectures and notes. Human needs are universal, and acknowledging our needs is empowering.

---

* See also the website of the Centre for Excellence in Universal Design: https://universaldesign.ie

Neuro Navigators in Families

'Urgh, you're so weird!' My little sister, hands on hips, accusatory, sooo angry. And me here, with no idea what I had done – as usual. Her shoulders drop, embarrassed and let down by her big sister again. 'Why can't you. Just. Be. *NORMAL*?'

I didn't know why. I didn't even know how I was being that *was* wrong, it just seemed to be...*me*. I didn't fit – not with the kids at school, not even with my own family. I had sisters and I knew we were related – same hair, same eyes, same skin. We lived in the same house, had the same parents. But I was the bad one. Not on paper, on paper I was straight-A's, good as gold, church mouse. But in my heart? I knew. I disappointed them, I didn't fit. It wasn't a drama or a tragedy, it was just a fact. I was different, and I had known as long as I could remember. I felt the rolled eyes, the clenched hands, the sharp frustrated exhales. I was difficult, picky, negative, oversensitive, too sensitive. I made everyone's life worse. With my existence.

I was always a hard worker, driven by more than a need to please, more like a need to prove that I am, that I have *worth*... So, I made it my mission: Be Normal. Surely, it can't be hard

– everyone else can do it. I could hold in my hands, control my face, change my voice, I could sit still and 'be good' – I could do whatever was needed to prove that I was enough.

And I know now that all of that? That drive, that process, that energy? It represents a privilege and a curse. I had the privilege of being able to use energy to identify and work to hide what was different about me. If my hands wanted to flap, and an adult shot me a look, I would make a note: they're angry, so hands still. If I let out an excited squeal, and one of my sisters flinched and screwed up her nose, another note: not okay, so hold it in. Over time, I curated a subconscious list of rules on 'how to be normal' or more accurately, how to be less annoying, how to be more tolerable, *how to be loved*. But inside I was the same. I've learned to speak, to hold my body in uncomfortable ways, to hold my breath to live. And that's the curse. Because while I may appear one way on the outside, it is not who I am. And the harder I worked to be what everyone else wanted, the more pressure I was under to keep it up, and the more it all confirmed that being myself was never ever going to be an option.

Before I go anywhere, I check how close the nearest McDonald's is. I check the parking, I check the location layout, I know where the toilets are, the exits, I prepare for who is going to be there, what conversation topics might come up. I create and follow hundreds of personal rules, and I do this because more than anything, I am incredibly anxious. I protect myself by making the unknown, known. By lighting up the shadows.

Before my husband Paul goes anywhere, he checks how close the nearest McDonald's is. He checks the parking, the layout, he prepares the same way I do. But Paul is not autistic, he's not anxious. He's not super-selective about what he eats, or afraid of saying or doing the wrong things. He does these things for me. Because he loves me, and he wants the world to be smooth for me.

If you love or care for someone who has needs outside of the current system, you might be the same. When you eat, when you travel, when you simply leave the house, you notice when things aren't accessible, you check for hazards, you can't help it – you see the world through the eyes of the person you love and support. You are a neuro navigator. Because when you love or care for someone who is different in any way, it means changing the way you see the world, shaping the world for them. Not out of obligation or resentment, out of love. You know, if your partner is a vegetarian, guess what? You're not suggesting a steakhouse dinner.

When it's your child who is different, the emotions come in waves. Anger at the injustice, grief at the loss, fear for the future. But more than anything, for me, the strongest and longest-lasting emotion is *a drive to make the world better*.

Families are weird. Not just yours, not just mine, and not just because we all have such specific quirks and preferences, but because the whole idea is full-on. The idea that we take a bunch of different personalities, throw them together in a limited physical space and leave them to form relationships, rules, and lives with minimal support or guidance. Whether they are together because of love, blood, coincidence, or serendipity, it seems to me that families are an art form. Families are conducted, created, negotiated, and adapted over time.

And then there's parenting. For many of us, becoming responsible for another human being is a shock. Not the nappies, not the crushing weight of responsibility (although, Wow! to that). Instead? The bubbling up of Every. Unresolved. Issue.

You. Have. Plus, some you thought you'd figured out and a bunch of issues you didn't even know you had. Whether you're co-parenting, step-parenting, parenting by biology, design, or desire: Children present the single biggest opportunity for personal growth available on the planet.

> Kick-ass parenting is optional. You don't have to heal trauma, break intergenerational cycles, or work on yourself in any way. You can do the minimum. You can slide by. Skip the extra credit. Ignore the side quests. I mean, C's get degrees, right? Yeah, but I'm thinking you're like me: You want a better world for your children. And that means making a choice: To learn, to grow, and maybe – even as a side-effect? – make the world better for everyone.

Meeting needs

When it comes to neurodivergence in families, it's all about needs:

- understanding needs
- communicating needs
- fine-tuning lifestyle to meet needs.

Understanding needs

First up? Know that being human means having needs. It means being made of crispy bone with electricity, wrapped in ageing meat and skin. Being human means being vulnerable in every way, and having needs doesn't make you weak or less-than. It makes you human. We all have specific needs: food, love, growth, no one touching your stuff. And whether you're neurodivergent or not, you deserve to have your needs acknowledged (ideally, respected). Your autistic kid's need for quiet time is just as valid as your diabetic kid's need for insulin. We don't measure needs, we honour them.

Communicating needs

It's hard enough to navigate a neurotypical world when everyone in a household is on the same page, but with so many aspects of life to navigate, the tiniest splinter can feel like a log. So how do you support siblings, ease grandparents, and deal with extended family who just don't get it? Take a breath. You're playing the long game here. You are not going to change anyone's mind with nagging, explaining, or incessant educational links. You do it by lighting the way. Let your relationship with your child be your focus, and set an example by challenging norms.

Fine-tuning lifestyle to meet needs

Once you understand the sensitivities, preferences, and needs at play in your family, it's time to get creative. In the 'Home' section we'll go through creating an autism-friendly home step-by-step. You'll notice there aren't usually strict, one-size-fits-all strategies. Instead? Understanding what is needed. Finding what works and the best way to make it happen.

When you're fine-tuning your lifestyle to incorporate different needs, there are two goals: making life work for your family right now, and supporting your child into the future. Big picture, life-wise, what is important to teach your child?

Right now, it might seem important for them to be compliant and fit in. But do you want them to be an adult who plays small and stays quiet? Sometimes, the things that make your life easier today, will disadvantage your child in the future. So, suck it up. Let your kid be the one who expresses their needs, trusts their body, sets boundaries, and says no. Empower them, support them, and set them up for success on their terms.

Remember: When a neurodivergent person's needs are met, it is not 'special treatment', getting 'spoiled', or being 'babied'. It's actually as everyday (meh, even) as asthma medication or reading glasses. If a child gets braces, it's because they need them. If you have two kids and one gets braces? It's because they need them. What does the other kid get? They get the privilege of *not needing braces*. When you're figuring out the best ways to meet needs, it's not about making things 'equal' or 'fair', it's about doing your best to give every individual what they need, and the best shot at an awesome life. A family is a team. Every member of the team has strengths and challenges, and the family has limited resources (time, energy, money, creativity, knowledge) to work with. It's a balance that is personal for every family, based on their own specific value and priorities. No single member of the family is more or less important. And needs aren't bargaining chips or power moves. Ideally? Every family member understands and respects all of the gifts and differences in their home (and in the world).

Ableism in the family

A note about adult family members who don't get it. They may never get it. Try to inspire and educate them if you feel compelled to, but generally, one parent (or more!) who gets it truly makes up for the one (or more) who doesn't. Use your energy to create the home you want, the life you love. Don't waste it fighting a system that is designed for conformity, and don't waste it arguing with people who may never understand.

And as for explaining the people who don't get it to an autistic? Adults are responsible for their actions and attitudes. If you have the energy to grant them grace, up to you. But your child is your priority, so here's your choice: Your child's innate way of being, or the ego and comfort of an adult who chooses not to grow. Thoughtlessness and ignorance hurts, even if it comes with 'good intentions'. Being 'family' doesn't negate ableism. Trauma inflicted by a loved one is still trauma. So do not shrug or laugh it off, do not defend hurtful behaviour with 'they didn't mean it' or 'don't worry about it'. You are showing your child what is okay and what is not. (Plus, adults do not need – or deserve – to be excused or protected with so-called 'white' lies.)

Ableism is discrimination based on the belief that people with typical abilities are superior. It can be as blatant as insults, and as subtle as a stereotype. Ableism is seeing people with disabilities as damaged or expendable, and disability as something to fix rather than something that just is. Like racism, sexism, and ageism, ableism is insidious and can seep through in language, attitudes, and behaviours. *Internalized ableism* is when we project that ableism onto ourselves. For example, comparing ourselves to others, thinking we are inferior, defective, or not disabled 'enough' to deserve supports (basically my exact reaction to finding out autism is a disability).*

Take a breath. There is a way to do this that is honest as well as respectful. Consider a softened honesty that protects the dignity of both the autistic and the family member involved. For example:

'Grandma is only just learning about autism. She's got lots to learn about being autistic. She loves you very much and hopefully she will update her old-fashioned ideas. We'll let her know that you can keep your headphones on, because that's how you can enjoy the concert.'

'We're not going to see your cousins for Christmas this year because they're going to have it at the community hall. We'll miss them, but it's a bit loud and it won't be fun for us there. I'm sorry we're not going to see them. What we'll do is see them the week before, and on Christmas have a movie day at our place with all-you-can-eat nuggets.'

'What a shame for your mum that she's not ready to learn about autism because it's actually really

* Reprinted from my book *Autistic World Domination: How to Script Your Life*, Jessica Kingsley Publishers, 2023.

awesome! We'll have to be patient with her neurotypical brain while she catches up!'

Your child will face ableism their whole life. They will be called 'rude' for speaking the truth and 'antisocial' for protecting their energy. You can give them the tools to kindly but firmly call it out. Be brave and start now, while they're small. You don't have to be an expert or an educator, you don't ever even have to engage. But it can be useful to have some responses ready for common ableist remarks and situations. Keep it polite but firm: 'In our family we respect sensory needs' or 'Everyone has different brains and bodies.' Create your own list of go-to responses and practise calling out ableism. Here are examples to get you thinking:

Ableist remark	Go-to response
'What's wrong with your kid?'	'Nothing's wrong with them, they're awesome!'
'They don't look autistic.'	'Huh, and you don't look ableist.'
'You don't seem disabled.'	'Being disabled isn't a bad thing.' 'Many disabilities aren't obvious and that can make it hard for people to understand.'
'Wow, you're so brave.'	'I don't think it's brave to love my kid.'
'Everyone's a little bit autistic.'	'Yes, everyone has autistic traits, but that doesn't make them autistic.' 'You can't be a little bit autistic, that's like being a little bit pregnant.' 'Everyone gets cold, but that doesn't make them ice cream.'

cont.

Ableist remark	Go-to response
'They're so inspiring!'	'They're just doing the same thing as all of the other kids.'

You do not have to respond, and you don't owe anyone personal or medical information. Only call someone out if you feel safe and have the energy. You might prefer to address your child instead, 'They're asking that because they don't understand that being autistic is pretty cool!'

Home

What if you'd never been told anything about how a home *should* look? What if you'd never been given ideas like 'You can't eat in the living room', 'Don't jump on the bed', Vacuum every day', and what if you didn't have a million other rules and expectations running around in your brain? Imagine what your home would be like if it didn't matter what anyone else thought. If it was just up to you – what would your home be like?

It's time for human beings (neurodivergent or not) to truly take on the idea that normal is what we decide and what we create. That our identities no longer have to conform into binary boxes. Not genders, not brains, not homes, not anything.

It's not easy being in a world that isn't designed for you, and it's not easy to see someone you love struggle in a world that isn't designed for them. Hey, but you know what *is* easy? Listening to us. Believing us.

There are so many (awesome, sensitive, brilliant) autistics in the world, and we're all trying to figure out how to fit in and who we fit with. It's not always easy and can take a long time for many of us. That's why the best thing neuro navigators can do at home is help us to have a safe and happy space. To help us find every possible thing that feels 'right' to help support us in a world that feels wrong so much of the time. Music, games, movies, food, animals, hobbies, even colours or textures, fidgets, headphones, a weighted blanket – finding the little things can lead to finding bigger things, like ideas for study or work, common interests for friends, or just ways to be happy each day.

First up, start experiencing your home like an autistic. You can do this by directly asking the autistic in your life verbally, or by writing a note and giving us time to process. If this isn't possible, use observation. Watch our body language:

- What does it look like when we are happy and relaxed? Do we stim with joy? For example, sing, flap, spin, etc.
- What does it look like when we are anxious and stressed? Do we stim to soothe? For example, yell, flap, spin, etc.
- Where are we happiest at home?
- What do we move closer to? Away from?
- Do we flinch at sounds? Which sounds? Lights? Which lights?
- Do we tense up in certain situations? For example, when a phone rings, with visitors, certain smells, or times of day.

The shortcut to understanding how autistics experience your home is by involving us in the process as much as possible. Of course, we may not always know what we want – how can you know whether you like a weighted blanket unless you've had one before? But maybe you've slept under a pile of fresh laundry? Or maybe you prefer the floor to a bed? Let us know that our input, and our happiness and comfort, is important to you. This gives us the confidence to try new things, and the permission to be in control of our bodies and our spaces.

Take your time. Breathe. You're finding the right flow for your home, and that may not happen overnight. Going against the norm isn't easy – riiiight up until you realize that the norm is making your life harder! This is a lifestyle change and it's okay to pace yourself. You are breaking cycles that have existed for generations. This work isn't easy, but it can change everything!

Remember: Physical changes can be a quick fix – so you need to back them up with your attitude, reminding yourself of what you've learned here and why.

Some frequently asked questions:

- **What if someone doesn't like a change?** Don't do it! Change it back, try a different way. This is not about swapping one discomfort for another! This world is too magical to tolerate being unhappy when there is so much possibility and choice. The only reason to change anything in your home (in your world!) is because it works, or because it feels good.
- **What if I don't have any extra money to buy resources?** Changing your attitudes and beliefs may not take money but will require time, awareness,

and energy. If you're not ready for that, it's okay. But know that, either way, you will use energy. And you can spend your energy battling meltdowns, or creating a home that supports an autistic way of being. (Spoiler alert: Go for option b!)

- **What if I have money for resources?** If you have the privilege of being able to spend time, money, or energy on your home environment, there are lots of ways to level up. You can look at your physical location: Where do you live? The city? The country? Do you have a garden? What is the weather like? You can try out different kinds of sensory gadgets, you could home school or organize to work from home, you can use your new mindset to imagine an autism-friendly life, and go about making it happen, bit by bit. Just remember: There is not a resource, therapy, toy, or tool in the world better than being respected and validated by another person.
- **What if my home is not my own? (Living with others, etc.)** This is not about convincing people who don't get it or forcing one person's preferences on anyone else. Focus on what you *can* change, what you *can* control. Even if it is just your own room, one shelf, one small space that honours who you are can be enough for now.
- **What if there is more than one autistic in the home?** If there is more than one autistic in a home (and awesomeness does tend to attract!), the goal will be to meet everyone's needs with the most win-win strategy possible (compromising is the last option).

- **What if [insert name of other human] doesn't want to make changes to our home?** Ideally, our home would be a haven where people of all neuro types can flourish. In real life? Sometimes there's a partner who doesn't get it, a kid who doesn't want to change, a stubborn flatmate, or a grandparent who likes things 'just so'. This is looking for a win-win-win-win-win. You are a clever and creative human! Find a way to make it work, find some grey in the black and white (or better yet, some rainbow!). Go online, ask in groups, get advice! Have a kid that is loud and a parent who needs quiet? Try headphones. Allocated noisy times. Have a parent that like mess and a kid who wants tidy? Negotiate spaces for each.

Every little bit counts. Truly. Many autistics have grown up in a world that is hostile, grating, hard. But to have one person who gets it? To have one safe place? It is EVERYTHING. You don't have to be perfect to make things better.

The autism-friendly home formula

Current environment + Specific autistic = Outcomes

When you combine the current environment (events, context, content) with the specific autistic (sensitivities, preferences), you get the outcome. In other words, how we respond and communicate is a combination of what is happening around us, and either soothed or worsened by available physical/

mental/emotional resources. This formula lets us create an autism-friendly home that is perfectly designed and adapted to an individual's strengths and challenges, their sensory sensitivities, and functional preferences.

Our goal isn't perfection – the current world doesn't allow for that (yet!). Our goal is to minimize negative outcomes (meltdowns, shutdowns, burnout) and maximize positive outcomes (relaxation, recovery, autistic joy) to support autistics to have a happier life and develop greater optimism and resilience.

- Make a room checklist. You can use a floor plan of your space or list the different spaces. For example: Entrance, Hallway, Kitchen, Living room/Lounge, Bathroom, Toilet, Stairs, Bedroom 1, Bedroom 2, Garage, Other.
- Go through the checklist, take it room by room. Remember: You don't have to do an entire area in one go! You can choose one room or theme a week, or a month. Pick an area, or a task, one at a time.
- In each room or space of your home, take the checklist and focus in on the one specific theme from the list below. Note down anything you notice in that space. If possible, ask the autistic.
    - **Sensory:** Our senses determine our reality. Autistics have literally, physically different sensing and processing systems. This means that just because an allistic (non-autistic) doesn't see it, feel it, hear it, or smell it, doesn't mean it isn't true. So if you talk to an autistic about their

sensory reality, assume competency. If we say something is too bright, for us it is. If we say something is too scratchy, for us it is. Our truth is truth.

- **Visual:** What is the available lighting in this space? Could you consider different bulbs, glows, star, colour, or shape projectors? Are small, dark spaces available? Cosy nooks or corners? What images, colours, and designs are in the space?
- **Sound:** What sounds can you hear? What can an autistic hear? Consider the sounds that are in this space over a twenty-four-hour period: Appliances? Ticking? People talking? A neighbourhood dog? Plumbing or flushing? Phone or notification tones? Door knocking? What sound can you control? Music, white noise, movies, audiobooks, meditations? Where are the quiet spaces? Does everyone have enough alone time? Could headphones ensure everyone can listen to their preferred music or block out sound when necessary?
- **Smells:** Chemicals, foods, plants, perfumes. Remember: Autistics can have heightened senses and can smell things other people can't. Trust the autistic, always.
- **Textures:** The floors, walls, furniture, items in the room – how do they feel? How do they feel to feet, hands, skin, face, brain?
- **Temperature:** Heating/cooling, clothing, curtains, blankets, pillows, air flow.

- **Objects:** Spinning sculptures, hanging mobiles, toys, models, mirrors, fidgets.
- **Energy:** In this space, what gives energy? What drains energy?
- **Make the unknown known:** What are the routines and schedules in this space? Menus? Systems? Calendar? To-do's? Can you increase predictability? Make things visual: sand-timers, lists, or even photos or images of tasks. Who else has access to this space, and what are their needs?
- **Communication:** How do you communicate in this space? What communication takes place in this space? Where are the exits and entries?
- **Kitchen:** This is a key space where you can take nothing for granted. Does dinner need to be at the table? Can food be separated? Served in separate dishes? Can a small new taste be provided alongside a preferred food? Does dinner have to be a single meal? Ask: How could we make this happen? Is it possible?
- **Food:** Are preferred foods available? Give autistics the courage and control to try new foods by ensuring they have access to expected foods that they enjoy.
- **Practical:** Are there things to do and places to do them?

- Once you have evaluated the area under all appropriate themes, it's time to think outside the box.
  - How can we support recovery by reducing sensory/social pressures?

- How can we increase resilience by boosting autistic joy? Can we add interests? Change the sensory environment?

This is about trying things, being okay with not knowing. Question everything. Take nothing for granted. In Earth's recent history, left-handers were smacked, outspoken women were burned, neurodivergents were left in institutions, and gay people were imprisoned. Society changes when we do. We need to challenge all of our existing assumptions and systems. What was is not what will be, and we determine what works for who we are, and what we want in this lifetime.

'Urgh. Why can't you. Just. Be. *NORMAL*?' My little sister, my classmates, my (almost) everyone. I grew up feeling as though normal was the goal, the win, the gold standard. Thanks to my diagnosis, I've learned that lots of the things about me that I thought were 'wrong' or 'broken' were actually just me coping with a world that is louder, brighter, and more intense than it is for other people. There is no normal. There is what works for us. The same way someone with asthma needs an inhaler, autistics need the right kinds of peace and stimulation for our physical system to thrive. This can mean quiet time, routine, music, and as many other preferences and ideals as we can think of and make happen! There is no one way, no right way. People now are multi-spectrum, kaleidoscopic. For so many of us, identity is a journey and it is huge. We are being diagnosed as neurodivergent late, we are connecting with our culture as adults, we are choosing to shape our life without the burden of some arbitrary 'normal' that was never going to work for a species as diverse and dynamic as human beings.

People like to say we can't control the world, but we can control *our* world. We can decide our language, our environment, we can decide the people and the energy that surround us. We decide the world in our heads, and in our homes.

Your life is going to get better every day because now you know that making these changes isn't 'walking on eggshells', it's meeting neurological needs.

8 Neuro Navigators in Education

In your classroom, the autistics won't always be the ones who are melting down and flipping tables. Sometimes they are the child that is quiet, overly eager to please, or the one with the perfect answers. It's not always possible to identify an autistic or neurodivergent learner, but happily, you don't need to spot us to make a huge difference.

Awareness of neurodivergence is increasing across the population. This growing appreciation, along with more neurodivergent-led education, dissolving stereotypes, and greater access to formal and self-diagnosis, means difference is the new normal. And while classrooms have always been an important tool, openness to diversity means the best possible educational experience will be available to more learners than ever before.

Because, for a long time, school was best for book brains. Sit still brains. Absorb and repeat brains. The outcomes of an education system reflect the intention of that system, not the potential of the brain involved. We've been creating cookie-cutter cogs for a dying capitalist machine. And it is so exciting to be on the edge of this new world! You know, the more I learn about the different ways human brains experience and process the world, the more embarrassed I feel by all the ways I am obliviously privileged. This was driven home for me when I decided to study te reo Māori as an adult. I knew that learning the language of my ancestors would be challenging. I was anxious about the other people, the environment, the regular-leaving-the-house of it all. But not for a moment was I worried about the actual learning. Because I'm smart, right? As a kid I read the dictionary for fun. Once I hit school I raced through literacy programmes, nailed exams, aced essays. I was (still am) the weird kid, and my teachers liked me because I was hungry to learn, I was quiet, paid attention, always went waaaay over the top with projects. But I was also different. I didn't fit with the other kids, I hid in the toilets during PE and in the library at lunchtime. I passed out at every single sex-ed class and my stories wove a fair bit of blood and guts in with my epic vocabulary. It's amazing what can be masked by straight-A's.

When the system works for you, you don't question it. You settle down into your privilege. You expect success. For me, the reading and writing part of school was easy. Learning from books and working with words. I had no idea that I was advantaged simply by being a learner with the kind of brain the system was designed for. What a shock to find out there are ways of learning outside my comfort zone. My te reo Māori classes featured face-to-face demonstrations of knowledge, verbal assessments, hands-on activities, practical skills, even singing and dancing. Suddenly, I wasn't the top of the class or the teacher's pet. Suddenly, I was the minority. While my classmates thrived with the range of learning options, I was struggling. I couldn't keep up with the verbal processing, I was uncomfortable collaborating, I felt slow, behind, and anxious about learning for the first time. It was humbling. Could this be how others had felt next to me at school? How some students might still feel in classrooms now? *Iti nei, iti nei*, little by little, changes are happening.

This isn't about favouring a specific way of learning, it's about not having to choose at all. Schools with sensory spaces and land-based education,* classrooms with fidgets and wobble stools. Tweaks and tools that seem small but can be identity-affirming and even lifesaving for learners who feel disconnected. Right now, it's a quiet revolution happening thanks to determined kids, trusting parents, and open-hearted, innovative teachers. The autism kaleidoscope features a diverse range of traits and intensities, and is best supported with jewels and brain candy just as diverse. Because wriggling, subdued, zoned-out, or nine hundred miles an hour, neurodivergents have one thing in common: a new way of being in the world.

The pandemic has speeded up changes that have been simmering for some time. The growing desire for education that is holistic and community-focused, global yet personalized, home learning, unlearning, child-centred, innovative, online, bite-sized, flexible, remote. Throw in the abundance of passion and technology, and we are primed for revolution! Old paradigms are dissolving. New voices are coming through and being heard. But here's the thing: Teachers have never been more important. As role-models. As neuro navigators.

---

* Land-based education is Indigenous-led, and strengthens culture and community through connection to ancestral land.

And FYI: Teachers are already doing incredible work, and I'm not here to say, 'Do more!' 'Be more!' The load on human beings right now is already huge. And teachers, like nurses, hairdressers, beauticians – and anyone in a profession that cares for others – work from the heart and take on so much. They are also caregivers, guides, counsellors, cheerleaders, role-models, and a million other things. Teaching is a calling. It has to be. The rewards are not always immediate or abundant. Like the beautiful proverb, faith means planting trees you may never sit in the shade of. You are so valued and so important.

So, while you don't need to study neurodivergencies, read the latest research, or dish out foolproof strategies (spoiler alert: there is no one-size, all-good, perfect strategy anyway), there are so many things you can do that will change the world for learners and their families.

Here's the thing: Receiving information is the smallest part of what makes education so credible. Education is a way to release the power of true identity and growth, a place to find connection and self, a place to decide who you are and what you want to do in the world. Teachers don't just teach, they embody, they affirm, they create the future.

- **In pre-schools:** Providing safety and love. Being a happy place. Developing physical independence, communication, and connection. Expressing and validating emotions.

- **In primary schools:** Feeding curiosity, identifying virtues, problem-solving, and community.
- **In secondary education:** Providing opportunities for greater exploration of self and skills. Developing a sense of self in the world.
- **In tertiary education:** Deepening or changing focus. Specializing further, sharpening skills and smoothing.
- **In adult and ongoing education:** Meeting people where they are and opening possibilities.

With the right systems, attitudes, and innovations, we can release the full power of education to reach people where they are, and then take them to a place where anything is possible. How can our educational organizations actively support and celebrate differences for the strengths they bring? What if being multiply divergent could be considered key to developing education that works for every kind of brain?

With my own children, I have been honoured (and privileged) to experience teachers who are supportive, loving, experienced, and wise. Teachers who look for strengths and opportunities, who truly love our children, and who have helped us grow as parents (and as people). This isn't always how it goes. If you bump up against teachers who feel like obstacles, it's okay to save your energy. Sometimes, it can be more effective to teach children to handle ignorance, and to be tolerant of the intolerant. You can't turn on the light for someone who is happy in the dark.

Right now, autistic graduation rates are below average, autistic students are more often stood down from school, and for those of us who do make it through? Work environments are often neurotypically designed, socially thorny sensory nightmares. There are also the autistics who start tertiary programmes and don't complete them, who are overeducated for the job they end up doing, or who complete multiple qualifications without ever going on to work in the industry they are trained for. This suggests there is more than intelligence or skill at play. There is a disconnect between what neurodivergent students want to do with their lives, and what actually happens. But why? Anecdotally, a common theme is 'I love to learn, I love the work, the problem was *everything else*.'

So, what is this 'everything else', and how can we support neurodivergent learners and educators to navigate the neurotypical world so we, they, all of us, can harness the skills and energy of neurodivergent brains?

Autistics are wired up for intensity, and we are often able to hyper-fixate on our passions and interests. (Yeah, those things the professionals call 'obsessions' or 'inappropriate ways of playing' in autistic children actually make us dedicated professionals and razor-sharp specialists as adults.) Unfortunately, even if our interests survive a childhood of being pathologized and frowned-upon, many of us go on to then be broken in the education system. Whether it's from being mocked or rejected by others, feeling jolted by transitions, missing social cues, switching between activities, forced teamwork, working without big-picture understanding, or being talked down to, every day is an exhausting array of physical and emotional challenges. And then there is the sensory onslaught. For sensitive brains in a classroom, overwhelm and overload can build up over time or devour us all of a sudden. But both can send us into a stress response that (depending on our traits and wiring) can manifest in different ways:

- **Hiding:** Finding small, dark, confined spaces to squeeze into. Disappearing. Being absent.
- **Running:** Escaping the environment, twisting, fighting, or making excuses to get away.
- **Blocking:** Covering eyes or ears, wearing headphones or a hoodie, tucking up inside clothing, engaging our brains with multiple tasks or input.
- **Distracting:** Creating sounds or movements to help absorb the stress. This could be jumping, flapping, humming, talking. Whatever works.

It's hard for a neurotypical brain to imagine that something as (supposedly) small as a clothing tag, a stray hair, a humming appliance, or a change of perfume could agitate someone to breaking point. And that's the key: Knowing and believing that different brains experience and process the world differently. Kids grow up in the world with very little control or power, vulnerable to the whims and ideas of the adults around them. If they flinch at a sound, and their grown-ups are dismissive, they get the message: *My feelings don't matter*. Multiply this over thousands of daily interactions and the message becomes: *My feelings are wrong, I can't trust myself, and I am alone*. This is gaslighting (see the box below) on a scale that sees us question our entire way of being in the world. And when this happens to us again and again across different environments and relationships, we stop questioning because there is no question. We know: We are broken and do not belong in this world.

'You're being oversensitive.' 'That's not what happened.' 'It's not a big deal.' 'It's your fault anyway.' Gaslighting is communication that leads someone to question their reality and self-worth. The term is taken from the 1938 stage play *Gas Light* by Patrick Hamilton. In the play, a husband manipulates his wife into questioning her sanity so he can steal from her. When she notices the gaslights dimming, he denies and dismisses her concerns. Gaslighting happens when neurotypicals try to convince neurodivergents (knowingly or not) that their experience of the world isn't real.

Coming from a place of trust is so important, especially with kids, who may not have the experience or self-knowledge to advocate for themselves. This means allowing and validating their experience. This means letting go of what you consider 'loud' or 'bright' or anything else. You do not get to determine the experience of someone else, even if it doesn't seem logical, or doesn't seem right. Even if it is completely different to anything you or any other person you know has ever felt or expressed. Even if you have been teaching for decades and have taught thousands of students. Every human comes with a unique combination of traits, strengths, senses, and potential.

The person in front of you is your priority. You can make a difference to that one person, and sometimes it is as simple as believing them.

Strategies and supports for autistics are often based around main themes to ease anxiety: creating safety and making the unknown known.

- Creating safety:
  - **Sensory safety:** For example, make environmental adjustments that allow us to find sensory comfort or block sensory overwhelm (headphones, fidgets, safe spaces – quiet spaces).
  - **Personal safety:** For example, support us to know ourselves, to understand boundaries, and provide guidance on how to express what we need so we can be heard. Have educators and staff who are trauma-informed.
- Making the unknown known:
  - For example, find ways to ease transitions by establishing familiarity and maintaining routine. Simplify language, be direct. Allow time for processing and for us to ask questions and explore details (especially whys and hows). To a neurotypical brain this can seem as though we are being 'defiant' or 'challenging authority', but as always, it comes down to the way we are wired. We ask question to interrogate logic, to make the unknown known, and to keep ourselves safe. It comes from a lifetime of getting things wrong, missing the point, failing to understand or meet expectations.

Support with executive functioning can also make a huge difference to many neurodivergents. We can get caught up in detail, forget deadlines, mismanage our workloads, and wear ourselves out. Neurotypical nurturing is a nice to have, but not enough. Some universities offer autistic mentoring that can provide a framework for connection and support. Not to mention realizing that there are others like us can be a lifeline at any age (but ideally the younger, the better!).

What if we created learning environments where these sorts of supports are built-in? Universal supports? So, instead of creating tools, environments, classrooms (everything!) for the typical human, the majority, the least-needy-most-privileged, we were to start creating for the universal human. To meet the most needs with the simplest solution, and make it available to everyone. The universal human isn't less-than, they are all-possibilities, they have choices. For example:

- Offering remote options and video replays of lessons or lectures supports flexibility for both neurodivergent and neurotypical humans.
- Providing dimmer switches on lights allows individual control both for people who need intense light and for people who prefer low light.

The best part is this: Little differences accumulate. Any changes you make, any learning you do for an individual learner, will not only make a difference to your own growth and to the effectiveness of your classroom, but also to your organization, and ultimately, to our community, and the world.

What would it look like if we started thinking of autism as a cultural difference rather than a strictly neurological difference? The autistic culture has its own language and communication, food, humour, ways of being, and, until now, has been buried and oppressed in favour of teaching us how to be 'normal' when actually autistics are an entire culture of people plunged into an unfamiliar environment. What if we supported our neurodivergent students the same way we do our international learners? What if we adapted our communication the way we would for an exchange student or foreign tourist? We would assume difference, rather than incompetence. And the strategies? Rather than aiming to 'fix' or 'solve' autistic challenges, strategies would instead support both cultures to learn and adapt to each other.

As the famous 20th-century physicist Max Planck once said, 'When you change the way you look at things, the things you look at change.' When we see our role as neuro navigator, as learning another culture, there are so many subtle shifts.

Our mindset, the attitude that influences every element of our communication – the micro-expressions, the vocal changes, right down to language. Let's imagine seeing autistic students as being like international students – you support them to understand your culture while appreciating the cultural differences they bring to your classroom. Consider that an instant change in approach from frustration to curiosity.

Suddenly, pastoral care, mentoring, using clear and careful language, and support with timetables and scheduling are reframed. No longer seen as *neurodivergent supports and strategies*, they are considered part of a cultural navigation. This will boost the respect, the nuances, the care that goes into supports. Because suddenly, you are not fixing a problem, you are adjusting a lifestyle. This increases trust and connection between neurotypical and neurodivergent brains; it makes support strategies human strategies.

I was at an autism conference where the hand dryers in the restrooms were turned off (epic move, organizers! – putting an end to the bathroom roar that many autistics find overwhelming); however, the hand dryers were labelled with an apology for the inconvenience. But wait, *who were they apologizing to?* The majority, the neurotypicals. Supports are ideals, not inconveniences.

As I explained in my book *Autistic World Domination*, autistic masking is a set of strategies used by autistics to appear neurotypical. Masking can include facial expressions, words, body language, even life choices. Masking is a survival mechanism, and long-term masking leads to autistic burnout. Masking is one reason many neurodivergent people aren't found, diagnosed, or supported. So, a student may be neurodivergent and not want to share, or feel comfortable sharing, their diagnosis; or they may be neurodivergent and not know it themselves. So, what does this mean in classrooms? It means a diagnosis, or 'looking disabled' (whatever that means) cannot be how we determine who gets support. Often, a teacher can be the first one to approach a parent about the strengths or challenges they see in a child. And with so many people being diagnosed as adults, teachers can be working with learners before they have this understanding for themselves. As a role-model, as a leader, as a navigator during this pivotal period in a person's life, teachers can make a huge difference.

When teachers approach learners with an openness and curiosity, it allows for possibility. By knowing that someone may not feel comfortable sharing their diagnosis, their needs, or their identity, disclosure stops being an obstacle to support. You may be working with someone who is not even aware of their neurodivergencies. *Nō reira*, the role of a teacher becomes a soft place to fall, a facilitator and guide, a neuro navigator.

Yes, we can go through the strategies, we can bring in tools, we can shape our spaces, and read all the research, but always remember that it is *who you are* that makes the biggest difference. Your eyes, your expression. You exude your values, your attitude, and when you hold space for us through a lens of positive intention, we can feel it.

There are no *special* needs. There are needs. Learning needs, support needs, human needs. And what if we put those supports in place so well, so universally, that they are considered the default setting? Allowing all students to thrive, neurodivergent or not. This brings possibilities, and the potential to open education up even more – to attract more students, to keep more students, and to satisfy more students.

Teachers can be pivotal role-models at every level of education. You have the honour (and responsibility) of guiding people through complex and delicate transition times – from child to adult, from novice to professional. And during that time? You get to decide the teacher you will be and the difference you will make. You may be the only person in someone's world who truly sees them – be that teacher. You might be the person who notices neurodivergent traits and raises it with them in a way that is supportive and empowering – be that teacher. You may be the first one to see them for their strengths and to use language that fills their world with possibilities – be that teacher. The values of your classroom or organization will be carried by your students into their lives, and into the world. You make a huge difference to every student, with your words, your attitude, your language, and your kind eyes.

Teaching is a calling, a gift, a world-changing magic, and when you bring your whole self to your work, and to your life, you make it possible for the people around you to do the same.

Neuro Navigators in the Workplace

So, I'm under my desk at work. Crying. Again. I'm taking big, slow, shaking breaths, trying to hold it in, trying and failing. Again. My eyes are burning, my heart is thudding, and I'm replaying every second of the last hour. Every second of my whole stupid life. *Everything they said, everything I did. All the ways I got things wrong (again) and made things worse (of course). All the things I could've done, should've done. How I'm going to get through this meltdown, and how I'm going to recover from it. Why this keeps happening to me.*

As an undiagnosed autistic in the workplace, I spent years hating myself for being (somehow) both too much and not enough. I was only fired from one job, for pacing. It was behind the counter and between customers, but my pacing was 'stressing people out'. More often, I left jobs. The specifics were always different: I was too much, too fast, too honest, I did things 'my own way', worked 'too hard', I 'questioned the status quo'. But actually? It was always just a new version of the same story: I didn't fit. It didn't matter how good I was at the work, it didn't matter how much I tried to blend, I could never stay long anywhere. It was like I was in a different world to everyone else. And I couldn't bear it. I saw, heard, and felt things that no one else seemed to even notice. Some places, I'd cry every day, overwhelmed by sensory everything, confused by the social spiderwebs, the office politics, the unspoken rules that somehow everyone else knew we were supposed to pretend to follow but actually ignore. Other places? It was as simple as telling the truth. It was (is) like I have a physical reaction to nonsense; lies, hypocrisy, ethics, even wasted time can set me off. For me, whenever I started to feel uncomfortable (a manager's lack of integrity, a co-worker taking advantage) it was an inevitable slide to the end. I always felt like I couldn't win: If I spoke up, I was the problem; if I stayed quiet, I agonized.

My history of missing (supposedly obvious) signals means questions and details are my defence against future failings. The assumption I make or the answer I don't get now will be the hole I fall into later. So, I look for gaps, for possible confusion, probable ambiguity, any hint of conflicting or missing data. Take this (survival-driven) attention to detail with a genuine belief that fixing errors makes things better, and add to it a belief that the quality of the work is more important than any one person* and you get a string of genuine questions and a workplace incident waiting to happen.

Once I understood more about my autistic identity, the situation flipped. Nothing about my environment changed, but

---

* This belief is often clinically described as 'lack of respect for/awareness of authority' and can be incredibly threatening to anyone ego-driven, or invested in current ways. Throw in mixed social signals, and you'll often find autistics asking questions and infuriating people while having no idea at all that they're doing it.

everything inside me did. Suddenly, when I felt challenged in a workplace (Hmm, I think this is someone else's work... Ouch! They are teaching incorrect pronunciation... Wait, so why are two people with the same job being paid differently?), I was able to see how it related to autistic traits:

- my strong sense of justice
- my pattern recognition and attention to detail
- my need for honesty and truth
- my preference for direct communication
- my inability to let go of something until I understand.

So, instead of becoming uncomfortable and leaving these organizations, I was able to express my ideas and concerns (call out plagiarism, request cultural competence, ask 'difficult' questions). Then, based on their response, consider whether they deserved my awesomeness. I still left, but knowing that it was my choice and not my failings made all the difference.

The stats around autistic unemployment and underemployment are high: They steal possibility, they spread fear and prejudice, and too often they become self-fulfilling. Click-hungry media pieces either reek with pity for us (and our 'long-suffering' caregivers) or gush with praise for our inspirational existence. Hey, how about instead of feeling sorry for us or calling us superheroes, media challenge the systems that make superpowers necessary for us to exist? Media coverage is always hungry for the ways we struggle and overcome. I want to see headlines filled with autistic entrepreneurs, redesigning the world to suit their skills and preferences, innovating, and blazing new ways of working.

These stories are just as abundant, just as true, but they help change the stereotypes and myths around autism instead of reinforcing them.

Because here's the thing: an autistic can have all the qualifications, skills, and qualities an organization desperately needs, but as long as society stays stuck in love with neurotypical ways of being, autistic talent will stay underused and undiscovered. Let's start with recruitment. So many job vacancies read like a checklist of autistic kryptonite. Companies are looking for 'team players' who are 'flexible' with 'interpersonal' and 'communication' skills. Hmm. Instantly alienating autonomous autistics. The neurotypical recruitment process values neurotypical traits – eye contact, smooth social skills, ease in an ever-changing environment – because human beings, whether they mean to or not, look for *sameness*. It's that whole thing again: who decides what's normal or appropriate? The majority. And if you are in the (current) majority? You may not realize the sheer universe of privilege you enjoy. So being a neuro navigator in the workplace means that to appreciate the value of an autistic (of any human really, but particularly an autistic one) you have to confront your ego.

Your ego is the part of you that prefers comfort over growth.
Your ego is the part of you that won't back down – even in the face of facts.
Your ego is the part of you that wants power and control served above all else.
Your ego is the part of you that will parade naked

> downtown* at the urging of conformity, while the autistics yell, 'You're naked!'

It is ego that stops us asking whether any way other than 'our way' could be right or even valuable. For many years, doctors and educators have been working to 'teach autistics social skills' based on the idea that because we don't connect with others in a neurotypical way we must be deficient. Now research shows that the social skills of autistics are not deficient, they are simply not neurotypical. We have distinctly *autistic* social skills. For example, autistics can be more comfortable sitting alongside another person talking about an interest, but uncomfortable sitting across from someone, making eye contact and answering questions. Any guesses on why we usually underperform at a typical job interview?

Autistics tend to skip the social games, and the office politics, with a communication style that is direct and honest, even to our own (social) detriment. 'Do you want to go for coffee?' – 'No.' 'Do you enjoy your work?' – 'No, I work to pay rent.' Employers will always say they value honesty – until they ask for feedback and we give it.

And this is the real reason that more than 80% of autistics are underemployed – not because we lack the talent, skills, qualifications, or willingness to work, but because the current systems are built for neurotypicals. And whether they mean to our not, they are looking for familiarity and *sameness*. And no matter what we do, neurodivergents tend to come across as *different*.

---

* In the way of The Emperor's New Clothes. Not just random naked parading, that's up to you.

Now, neurodiversity has become a buzzword in the business world, and at one end of the spectrum (haha) it's just another tick-box for companies to signal inclusiveness. Of course, there are also organizations making the most of our strengths; these are the ones making an autism diagnosis a prerequisite of employment. They rearrange workspaces to make them autism-friendly, they offer workshops and paid test projects instead of interviews, they work with schools to ease transitions. This is across business-types from software companies and animation studios to factories and corporate offices. Seriously. Because they know that, in the right environment, autistics are loyal, hardworking, honest employees. They've realized we're not only great at repetitive tasks, error spotting, and problem-solving, but also? We don't lie, we don't pretend, we don't take as many sick days. Suddenly, an autism diagnosis is a way to source the best employees. This means money is being spent to analyse and take advantage of making neurodivergent brains more comfortable. While this sounds like a good thing, be wary. Are autistics being hired across the company, or only in certain roles? Are we good enough in darkened computer labs, but not as leaders? Are existing neurodivergent employees happy and respected in their roles? Actually *being* inclusive is more important than appearing inclusive. Worst case? This 'Yay Autism!' can be as exploitative and harmful to the autistic community as the non-profits' fundraising to 'cure' us. The ideal sits somewhere between pitying oppression and world domination: for neurodivergents to be as valued and respected as any other human. (Although, I would certainly welcome autistic overlords. A world run by autistics* could see a much-needed injection of values such as truth, justice, and tagless clothing.)

There is a lot of ego and money invested in the status quo. So, when it comes to the workplace, I have a heap of optimism but not a lot of trust. I would love to believe that people will drop their ego in favour of what's right for the work, I would love to champion the hardworking DEI departments, and promote the new, neuroaffirming ways of the world. But I'm also conscious of my privilege. The progress I see and feel in the world has a long way to go to trickle down into everyday life. For most autistics right now, particularly adult and undiagnosed, making a living means surviving neurotypical systems. Because as much as autistics benefit the workplace with our efficiency, hyper-focus, honesty, and innovation, these traits are, more often than not, disadvantages to our own health and wellbeing. And many autistic traits also leave us vulnerable to manipulation and abuse. In the workplace, this can look like:

- feeling overly responsible (and taking on blame that isn't ours)
- speaking up for injustice (even when those around us know it's a social mistake)
- correcting errors and finding mistakes (unaware others are being offended)

---

* Disclaimer: Autistics are kaleidoscopic trait-wise, like any human. We aren't innately angelic and we have our weaknesses. This is more about implementing neuroaffirmative systems and leadership. Exploring ways of doing things that empower more (if not all!) humans, not just winners of the postcode-neurotype-gender-ethnicity-ability lottery.

- completing other people's work (not realizing we are being taken advantage of).

I'm one of those autistics that appears neurotypical, and what that means is that you can't see how hard I'm working. Obviously, you can't know what you don't know, but there are ways you can instantly make it easier for the neurodivergents in your workplace, whether they share their identity publicly or not. It's by dropping your norms, assumptions, and expectations. By holding respect and assuming positive intention for the people around you. For example, consider the norms, assumptions, and expectations of these work situations:

- A person who is often late. (Disorganized? Lazy? Unmotivated?)
- A person who prefers a specific work desk. (Picky? Difficult? Arrogant?)
- A person who doesn't attend Friday-night work drinks. (Unfriendly? Antisocial? Not a team-player?)
- A person who scribbles during meetings. (Bored? Distracted? Uninterested?)
- A person who brings up errors and issues. (Annoying? Negative? Depressing?)

We know that between neurodivergencies, personal preferences, life challenges, and a million other variables, human beings are complex. Let's at least choose how and what we assume. Let fresh possibilities melt away what you think you know.

- Could a person be late because they experience

executive dysfunction? Or because they are responsible for someone who does?
- Could a person prefer a specific work desk because of sensory sensitivities? Overwhelm?
- Could a person skip Friday-night work drinks because they have social anxiety? Because they have home or personal commitments? Could they be avoiding alcohol?
- Could a person who scribbles during meetings be using it as a sensory tool to increase focus? Could they be expending excess energy while trying to sit still and appear neurotypical?
- Could a person who brings up errors and issues be thinking practically? Finding ways to safeguard success? Could they be someone who has made mistakes in the past, or been responsible for fixing other people's mistakes?

You don't need specialized knowledge to treat every person with respect. You don't need inclusion workshops to approach situations with an open heart. Like every kind of prejudice or shadow, you change it instantly with consciousness and light. The challenge is identifying privilege that you don't know you have. The shortcut is to truly believe that there is more than one right way to be human and then be willing to replace your automatic responses (and genuinely apologize and make amends when you get it wrong).

This is how inclusion and belonging becomes business-as-usual, not with policies or tick-boxes, but by changing ourselves. Now. By getting clear about the values and beliefs we ooze. By actively being better. By educating yourself and (if you are lucky enough to receive it) accepting feedback from outside your neurotype (your gender, your age, your ability...) as not only fact, but GOLD. By making change, not sometime, one day, if we can, when we can, but NOW. In every moment we are creating spaces where people can (and want to!) bring their genuine whole self to work. Whether it's a physical space, a mental space, or an emotional one. We choose to create space. We can choose to make inclusive systems the bare minimum, the launch point for excellence. We can make sure that people get the support that works for them without having to prove they 'need' them, or even request them. And this makes financial sense too, because full inclusion means we can get to every individual's strengths faster – not waste time on challenges that we have the resources to minimize. Let's make it all available: remote and flexible working, neuro-affirming physical spaces, captioning, IT, the way we manage time, technology assistance, environments where accessing support and having needs met is upfront and simple. Wait, what if everyone starts to want wobble chairs and fidgets? What if all offices had soft, adjustable lighting? Or everyone wears headphones and sunglasses? Oh no, a happier, healthier, more productive team! The horror! #Sarcasm.

While lots of workplaces are getting it, many more are not. So my advice to workplaces and actual autistics is very different.

My advice to organizations is: Do the work. Hire neurodivergent educators and consultants. Make sure that your actual hiring practices and systems are neuroaffirming, not just your hopes and intentions. Examine your beliefs about what it means to be human, to be normal. Acknowledge your privilege and as much as possible, lead from the top.

But to autistics? My advice is to put yourself first. If you're not happy, find another job and leave as soon as you can. Obviously, not everyone will have the privilege of leaving work the way I did, or working for themselves, but understanding it's 'them not you' gives you a far healthier perspective than feeling constantly broken and out of place. As the bumper sticker says, 'Before you blame yourself, make sure you are not just surrounded by jerks'. (Disclaimer: Taking responsibility is different to blaming yourself. One is owning up to your actions, the other is beating yourself up for them.) There is a place where you belong, and where your strengths are strengths. Holding on to this faith is self-care in a world that is run by neurotypicals (for now).

Discover your strengths, find what you love, and figure out ways to survive the neurotypical world with enough energy left for whatever brings you joy. Our intensity makes us vulnerable as well as incredible. So, yes, if you find a traditional job that looks like it could work for you – do the research. Talk to existing or past employees, be ready to ask for what you want; and if you have the confidence and the privilege – be ready to say no and tell them why. But don't jeopardize your own health or energy to bless a workplace with suggestions or ideas that they fight you on. It may well be less energy to hold it in, hold yourself together, and just get through your days. Find your joy and focus there. Because even though you are in charge of your world, you are not responsible for the entire world. You deserve to breathe, and you deserve the best possible world for you.

And Finally: The World Is Changing

Ultimately, big picture, long term, the neurodivergents will run the world. We will. The world will be designed by and for us, and you know what? The neurotypicals will be happier for it. This is because being sensitive, being open, and being free is innately human. As the neurodivergent population grows, so does respect and understanding across individuals, communities, and the systems of our current world. All people are sensory beings, easily affected by our environment; neurodivergents are just more finely tuned and feel it sooner. We are the canaries in the coalmine. Ignore us and you're next.

Meanwhile, we're not waiting any longer. We're done arguing. We're not here to fight the system to create what is obvious to us. We're not going to waste energy dismantling darkness, because we are bringing the light. Every change, every voice, every moment of joy pokes a hole in the darkness, lets the light in.

Neuro navigators are shaping the world, for ourselves and for our loved ones. This means we are doing it from a place of power and knowing, and more than that? The purest love.

One parent can be ignored, one caregiver can be brushed aside, one manager can be debated, one professional can be diminished. Divided we are minorities, but all of us? Together? We have one voice with the same message: Our world deserves better. We're not going to wait for the rescue, for permission, for the system to change. We're already there, we're doing it now. We are connecting, learning from each other, becoming one voice and one light. Because science and technology is not the leading edge, the leading edge is our hearts, our knowing, and the spark of our ancestors – our humanity. I am honoured and proud to be with you and to be one of you. We are creating a world that no longer needs to be navigated.

Glossary

Ableism is discrimination based on the belief that people with typical abilities are superior.

Autism is a way of being in, processing, and experiencing the world. Autistics experience the world intensely, with preferences for a selective social circle, intentional and neurodivergent communication, consistent routine, and favourite things (music, food, movies, textures, etc.). A te reo Māori way to express autism is *takiwātanga* meaning in my/his/her/their own time and space.

Executive function and self-regulation are mental processes that enable us to plan, focus attention, remember instructions, and juggle multiple tasks successfully.

Intersectionality (coined by law professor Kimberlé Crenshaw[9]) acknowledges that the different aspects and identities of each person layer and combine to create different forms of discrimination, disadvantage, privilege, and oppression.

Masking means the strategies used by autistics to appear neurotypical. Masking can include facial expressions, words, body language, even life choices. Masking is a survival mechanism activated by stress, and long-term masking leads to burnout.

Multiply divergent is when a person has more than one neurodivergence. For example, people can be Indigenous and gifted, or have Tourette's and a brain injury. These combinations can make diagnosis more complicated and identity more complex, but offer incredible magic and insight in creating a new world.

Neurodivergent and neurodivergence were coined by Kassiane Asasumasu and mean neurologically divergent from typical. Neurodivergent excludes being neurotypical.

Neurodiversity is a biological characteristic of human beings. Coined by Judy Singer, it describes the diversity of brain function across all people. Neurodiversity includes being neurotypical.

Stim is short for 'self-stimulation'. A stim is a movement or sensation that is repeated to relieve stress. Autistics also stim because it feels good! Stims can be physical, auditory, visual, tactile. Stimming brings autistic joy!

Universal design is making spaces, products, and systems usable by every kind of human. Everyone. The term was coined by architect Ronald Mace. Also known as inclusive design, and barrier-free design.

Whakataukī (Māori proverbs)

The legs of the rainbow stand in two different places. *Āni-waniwa tū wae rua.*

The tītoki tree blooms in its own time. *He wā tōna ka puāwai mai te tītoki.*

Words have power. *He mana tō te kupu.*

A rock in the ocean. *He toka tū moana.*

Endnotes

1 Opai, K. (n.d.) Te Reo Hāpai. The Language of Enrichment. www.tereohapai.nz

2 Singer, J. (2020, 12 August) What is wrong with this Wikipedia definition of neurodiversity? [Blog post]. Reflections on Neurodiversity. https://neurodiversity2.blogspot.com/2020/08

3 sherlocksflataffect (2015) PSA from the actual coiner of "neurodivergent". *Tumblr*. https://sherlocksflataffect.tumblr.com/post/121295972384/psa-from-the-actual-coiner-of-neurodivergent

4 Miserandino, C. (2010) The Spoon Theory. But you don't look sick. https://butyoudontlooksick.com/articles/written-by-christine/the-spoon-theory

5 Wansink, B. and Sobal, J. (2007) Mindless eating: The 200 daily food decisions we overlook. *Environment and Behavior, 39*(1), 106–123.

6 Ibid.

7 Milton, D.E.M. (2012) On the ontological status of autism: The 'double empathy problem'. *Disability & Society, 27*(6), 883–887.

8 Crompton, C.J., Ropar, D., Evans-Williams, C.V., Flynn, E.G., and Fletcher-Watson, S. (2020) Autistic peer-to-peer information transfer is highly effective. *Autism, 24*, 1704–1712. doi:10.1177/1362361320919286

9 Crenshaw, K. (2017) Kimberlé Crenshaw on intersectionality, more than two decades later [Interview]. Columbia Law School. www.law.columbia.edu/news/archive/kimberle-crenshaw-intersectionality-more-two-decades-later